Are You Agité?

A Treatise
on Everyday Agitation

Philippe Trétiack

Are You Agité?

A Treatise
on Everyday Agitation

Algora Publishing
New York

Algora Publishing, New York
© 2000 by Algora Publishing
All rights reserved. Published 2000.
Printed in the United States of America
ISBN: 1-892941-09-0
Editors@algora.com

Originally published as Traité de l'agitation ordinaire© Editions Grasset & Fasquelle, 1998.

Library of Congress Cataloging-in-Publication Data

Trétiack, Philippe.
  [Traité de l'agitation ordinaire. English]
  Are You Agité? : A Treatise on Everyday Agitation / by Philippe Trétiack.
     p. cm.
  ISBN 1-892941-09-0 (alk. paper)
  1. Agitation (Psychology) I. Title.
  BF575.A35 T7413 2000
  155.9—dc21
                              00-009211

Algora Publishing
wishes to express its appreciation
for the assistance given by
the Government of France
through the Ministry of Culture
in support of the preparation of this translation.

New York
www.algora.com

Table of Contents

Where Do We Stand?   7

PART ONE: The Agité at the Mercy of Fashion   11

1. In the Jaws of Acceleration   13

2. The Melancholy of the Agité   63

PART TWO: The World at the Mercy of the Agité   77

1. The Agité as a Seismograph   79

2. The Agité in the Rat Race   119

3. Nerves!   133

PART THREE: The Agité Goes on the Attack   165

1. Hair-Trigger Agitation   167

2. Agitated in Every Sense   193

To the devilish trio:

Odile Decq, Benoit Cornette and Francis Rambert

"For years, Moscow had been living
in an impossible state of precipitation.
Everyone was running, gushing, jumping —
shouting "See you later!," "Hi!"

AKSYONOV

A Moscow Saga

In the introduction to his *Images in the Margins: At the Fringes of Medieval Art*,[1] Michael Camille extends an invitation to the reader: feel free to fill the margins with a spidery scrawl and doodlings, like the copyists hunching over in the chill air of the cloisters; decorate it, in your own way, with notes and comments; illuminate it!

I say the same, and I add: may you handle this book in your own usual agitated way. Throw it around, abuse it, shake it as the imperial one in Calcutta shakes his dhotis, his saris and his flies. May this book be read in the cargo compartment of a Cathay Pacific Boeing 747, in a taxi heading for JFK Airport, on a jet-ski splashing over the Caribbean, in the slums of Marseilles, on the beaches Waikiki, in a rickshaw, a junk or a palanquin; may it be stuffed in pockets and plastic bags, suffer the insults of a river in rut, bounce out the top of a convertible and tumble across the highway, sop up a spilled cup of coffee. May this book be dynamited. It will recover the freedom that the yoke of the binding has stolen from it.

---

1. Gallimard, 1997.

WHERE DO WE STAND?

I'm agitated. Obviously. Everybody tells me I am. They tell me all the time. "How do you get so much done?" "You're so lucky!" "When do you sleep?" Every time, underneath the cheery talk is a little jealousy and considerable condescension. All those jealous sidelong glances, snide little smiles, everyone so sure of himself. "He's a good guy, that Trétiack, but a lightweight, superficial, no staying power."

In the end, this ticks me off, I confess.

So I am writing for that multitude, the army of the active, those who dance an electric jig. Those whose feet are tapping under the table, whose lungs swell with a surfeit of energy, whose eyes blaze with dynamic drive. I see them, I recognize them, I know them. They are everywhere. The airports are full of them, the streets are teeming with them, the avenues are jammed with them. I see them jumping from train to taxi, from one subject to another, spinning off ideas for new deals and new adventures, drowning in plans. They don't look unhappy. Propelled, rather, and pleased with what is happening to them. A life of the unforeseeable, daily surprises, questions, diversions and new starts. Who would complain about that? Good God, to escape the bureaucratic blahs, to run your own business on the side (and sometimes two or three), gold-bricking, doing something that you enjoy. . . These people have lovers, mistresses, who knows what-all?

And still. Listening to them talk, you would think they were cursed, sick. They complain, they cover up, they don't dare to enjoy too much in public. In short, they feel guilty about racing, ashamed of this abundance of life . . . the false modesty that is imposed on them!

This book, born of dissatisfaction, of a neurotic impulse, is a defense of nothing more nor less than our way of being — always on the go, always on the look-out for what's new. A defense and an illustration of Agitation as a state of jubilation. And don't anyone try to tell me that I have written a treatise on happiness. That's not it. Jubilation has nothing to do with being happy or unhappy, because it has nothing to do with sin; no, Agitation has nothing to do with anything but the pleasure of being agitated. True, it sometimes happens that this pleasure can cause trouble, can wound and lead to suffering. It can also be simple euphoria. It depends.

This *Treatise on Everyday Agitation* does not hide any of the realities of these multiple states. Yes, there is something ridiculous in Agitation; it sets you up to be caught by the whims of fashion, the siren song of an appealing commercial, the latest fad, a limited series, the most recent "must-have." Yes, to be *Agité* can sometimes be quite ridiculous. Yes, the exaltation of agitation sometimes has a whiff of narcosis, a drug. Yes, you can burn yourself if you get too close to the fire. Yes, the Agité is a depressive, in a state of lack, haunted by the collapses that inevitably follow the highs. Under every Agité there lurks a melancholic (but still furious) person; that's a fact that is as old as the world. You'll find all of that in this *Treatise* (a handbook for the person with a finger in every pie); for that is his daily fare.

On the other hand, the *Agité* opposes the *diktat* of channel flipping. Yes, he keeps his hand on the remote control, but no, the *Agité* is not a "zapper," he is his sworn enemy. The zapper is always disappointed, stomping off on an infernal pursuit, one dead end after another, a labyrinth of emptiness leading to more emptiness. The *Agité*, on the other hand, is exalted, skipping from one excitement to another. If he jumps from one thing to the next it is out of curiosity, not disenchantment.

And then. Then? All the rest. In a world of constant acceleration, you have to be on the move to catch the wave. *Agitation* is a way of seizing reality and of recreating it, and a means of resisting it and of perverting it as well, of being (to some extent) its seismograph and sometimes its lightning rod. Taking a

100,000-volt shock or falling in love at first sight: it's a risky business, a matter of timing. *Agités* want it. They want it all. Is that why people are upset with them?

And now, it's your turn to play. Do you have a touch of the dervish syndrome? Do you see the contemplative person as nice, pleasant, but totalitarian and, in short . . . a pain in the ass?

Let's do a check-up. If it so happens that you:

— eat your lunch while clearing the table, or without setting the table in the first place;

— dial your car phone while changing lanes;

— burn yourself taking things out of the microwave without a potholder;

— read the newspaper while watching TV;

— stop in at Bloomingdale's too often, just to look;

— start one book and then another, and a third and a fourth;

— pile up magazines and newspapers in the increasingly hypothetical hope of reading them one day, "when you have time";

— consistently arrive early, or late, because your schedule is out of control;

— feel exalted without any specific reason;

— possibly have an extra-marital liaison; or two;

— pursue three hobbies that get in the way of your profession, and keep getting over your head in new plans. . .

it's because you are part of the great network of *Agités*.

But does that make you unhappy?

Part One

THE *AGITÉ* AT THE MERCY OF FASHION

1.

In the Jaws of Acceleration

Hounded by the ephemeral and the effervescent, buffeted by sudden fads and fashion trends, the Agité flits about. Subject to the dictatorship of overabundant supply, moved by a diabolical instinct to mastery, he throws himself headlong into everything that scintillates. At the risk of dissolving, he wants to be everywhere at once, to miss nothing in the world that erupts, innovates, rocks. Guilt stalks him.

His bulimia is a neurosis, his shivers are the beginning of nausea.

Welcome to the Ballistic Society

Zap, move, juggle, skip, stop, keep moving forward, smash the doors, take the hits but keep going, go, go, go until the KO. Clear things out, weed things out, take the alternate route, choose the three-phase current, the electrified, electronic, hypertonic, cyberspace; don't accept any but the maximum tension, a stridency of explosions; don't put up with yourself, hate yourself, consider yourself in revolt and even in revolution, constantly feel the rush, the over-excitement; slam the doors, shout in the staircase, be already gone, always missing, a dictator by escape, an autocrat by humor. Crush the accelerator, smash the floor, twist the pedals, make the engine howl and the cylinders whine, burn out the motor, rip the sheet metal, keep going faster and never stop; run out of breath, catch up with your era, go beyond it, never age.

There was a time when intellectuals suffered from melancholy. Nowadays, they are going ballistic. They have substituted acceleration for languid romanticism. Our lives are trajectories. Human ray-guns in a society where "zapping" has become a watchword, all of us, the Agités, exalted, inspired and propelled from one enthusiasm to another, we are digging our tomb. They accuse us of being nothing but eclectic weather-vanes sick with the intoxication of the dilettante, automatic victims of the race for superficiality where just-about-everything is equivalent to anything-at-all, which is itself the post-modern form of nothing-at-all. The contemplative ones, those who are so self-controlled, have us pegged. The vote is in. The wise, respectful verdict has been returned; we are convicted. The philosophers, the specialists, they scorn the eclectics, the Agités.

And what if they're right? And if, from a spasm to a convulsion, subjected to the dictatorial, totalitarian pressure of zapping, we have already lost the ability to think? Just animated reflexes, feverish, predators quick to jump on "the latest rage," "the hottest thing," the ultimate craze! Mired in the acknowledged impossibility of living up to any pretense of being avant-garde, unable to fight against the current, reduced to mere instinctual activities, victim of the soup merchants, is the Agité that I am slave to so many gadgets?

Do the jerks, the accelerations, the drug of travel, the requirements of compressed time, being stuffed to the gills, still permit a thought of chewing that is not stamped "fast-food"?

Too Many Women, Too Much Money, Too Fast

Ten years ago the biography of Hugh Hefner, the legendary owner of the magazine *Playboy*, was published with that as its intoxicating and indisputable subtitle.[1] The man who had built an empire where the legions wore bunny ears, and furry tails on their buttocks, was clearly fed up. No one in the history of the universe had had to slump in so many ridiculous armchairs day after day, sipping cognac and bourbon, wearily caressing the rounded rumps of his geishas, displaying his hairy chest like a military decoration for photographers who obliged him to change his dressing gown with every roll of film. An entire life carried out under the aegis of bad taste. In a paradigmatic way (that one cannot help but envy), this genius of a jerk was the victim of a nauseating century.

With so many primal forces tugging at his sleeve, titillated nonstop by so many prizes arrayed within hand's reach (so to speak), this guy knew the horror of constant satiety, the insomnia of the bed linen merchant, the confectioner's nausea. Formerly reserved for the pasha, for the affluent, this contemporary evil now strangles John and Jane Doe. Even without a lover, and with no money to spare, ordinary people are deluged by fantasies that subjugate them, that are instilled in them, that are imposed on them. Desires, needs, requirements. Like everyone, they suffer not for want of ideas but for the incapacity to distinguish them, to arrange them hierarchically. Every morning for some, every hour for others, a conglomeration of thoughts invades their consciousness, insists, and forms a foul brew. In a few years' time, we have made the leap from a society of material excess to that of excess in every sense.

While there is plenty of reason to vomit at the accumulation of goods thrown in our faces, this feeling of aversion doesn't even take into consideration the guilty feelings prompted by the juxtaposition with dire poverty. The poor wretches of Bangladesh and Mogadishu, mobs that yesterday were hidden from view, have crowded into our subways and our stairwells in vain: it is not the contrast of wealth and misery that disturbs us but our own incapacity to ingest, much less digest, everything that is presented to us. We are so well "served" that it makes us uncomfortable. It's the "supermarket" effect, embodied to the ultimate degree by the megastores. Such a name should already make us hit the road. Run away. Flee. But no. We go, and we shop. In the mass of customers squeezing their way through parking lots overflowing with "compacts," we each, in turn, shove our way in, find something, and squeeze together at the cash registers; but who has not had an uncomfortable feeling, looking at all those CD's, all those books, all that glistening culture that is escaping us? The phenomenon has reached the saturation point. It more and more often turns to sheer frustration. Buying a book isn't a matter of giving oneself the pleasure of reading it, anymore, but a recognition of the cruel reality of all those other books that we will never have time to read. A quick perusal of the bookcases piling up at home is enough to prove that it's no use stuffing them fuller still. We collapse in suffering under the overflowing shelves, under the piles of discs and videos. A suffocating accumulation. Time is scoffing at us. No, you will never have the leisure to listen to all the wonders that make your shelves sag. No. And especially not, since you waste precious hours in other stores looking to buy still more.

What you would need, what we all need, what should be required, obligatory, is a massive inventory close-out sale, like at the big discount stores. A vain hope. Accumulation seems to ward off death, and we like that, it perks us up. So in moments of great distress, when the weight bears down on us,[2] we have to adopt survival techniques.

The Agité who — despite everything — haunts the bookshops, gets hooked, picks up a new book here and there, a catalogue, a disc by some group that is smashing the charts, is governed by the anguished impulse that forbids him to control his itch to buy. He is gripped by the instinct to have and to know everything. He is caught, he is trapped. Moreover, in the space of a few months, France has been covered with "Cash Converters" and other barter-based chain store franchises. In these "new look" retail shops, halfway between *Dallas* kitsch and post-Chernobyl sordidness, fanatical consumers on their way to the poorhouse can sell off their television sets and their food processors for "money, cash paid immediately," in order to get second-hand CD players and laptops. "We sail on the irrepressible wave of over-consumption among the poor," summarizes a leaflet from a "re-sale shop." Their turnover rate is exploding. The instinct to have it all is a drug. The Agité wants to get a fix but his enthusiasm always leads to a dead end. Neurotic agitation is a misery.

Everything is New, Even the News

The world is not a world any more but a tide of information. Every second challenges us to acquire, to receive, to ingurgitate, to take in the full import of another bit of news, another piece of data, a crucial scoop, an instance of total ineptitude. The sin of being ill-informed has become a throbbing torture. A piercing awareness that we are missing things, and a constant state of the "near miss," a palpable collision with nothingness. An embarrassment of fleeting riches. We have to know, to know everything, immediately. The drama of a situation that binds us in blinding proximity. And Agités allow themselves to be taken prisoner. Their craniums dilate, expanding like Jiffy-Pop under the impact of so many exploding factoids.

The brevity, the speed of change, the weight of the "information" does not leave them any chance of keeping the least distance. Of course, that is the secret of any good story, any re-write, any imaginary presentation, any artistic process. In the heat of the action, what should you grab hold of? Nothing. The most lucid just rely on themselves, but as for the event that they are experiencing, there is nothing to hold onto but ashes! When unknown gunmen have taken over the main intersection, when you find yourself caught in the middle of a shoot-out, when a bomb explodes just a hundred yards away — which happened to me in Ankara, in 1985 — you don't understand anything any more. You get a flood of past experiences, a flashback more than a trip. The deluge of information, and the injunction to constantly suck in more information, are explosive. A permanent state of alarm.

French Doctor

The success of the *Emergency Room* series is no accident. It is an indicator. In the 15th century, Filippo Brunelleschi with his *camera obscura* device gave birth to perspective, to the plan. The long-term emerged from his box with its inverted mirrors. Today that mirror is broken. Perspective has given way to the network, the grid, the instantaneous, the short-term. The feeling of urgency is becoming omnipresent, ostentatious, obsessive. In the humanitarian realm, above all. Act instantly, wherever the wound opens. Give relief, to relieve yourself. Cure, cleanse, curette, prevent? We haven't got the time or even the idea. The Renaissance is behind us. Death is on all sides. So Agités parachute from Sudan to Armenia, Kabul to Medellín. They apply bandages. They cleanse sutures. They apply compresses for compressed time.

Don Juan, playboy, lady's man . . . Adultery-Circus. Exacerbated schizophrenic modernity makes my mouth water, teasing my tastebuds with so many savory promises; so many costumes to try!

Marguerite Duras: "With one woman, you know all women." In the present context of so many temptations, is that, for one instant, credible?

Too Much, Always Too Much, Too Much All the Time

Cram. In Great Britain, the latest big hit in men's journalism is called *Loaded*. In other words "charged," "full," "stuffed." With alcohol, money, women. A whole program that expresses the intoxication of accumulation. Plastic bags frantically hoarded by men and women alike, stuffed under sinks, piled up behind refrigerators, jammed into other plastic bags; stockpiles of dust, of nothing, of the unclassifiable. So, lacking confidence, Professor K., the brains behind the radical magazine *Citizen K*, shifted to confessions. He exposed everything. His interest in inventions, futurology, the future, his constant desire to know what tomorrow will be like, are all a skillful way of masking his lack of culture. Because he doesn't know enough about the past, because he did not devour the classics, did not strain his eyes enough under a lamp reading some arid treatises, he thinks that by running ahead he can keep everyone from daring to ask for a background check on him. Move fast to prevent any interruption, any verification. Moreover no one, or almost no one, is suspicious. Simply, they are wary about him. By getting involved in everything, he leaves himself exposed to everything; by touching on everything, he becomes untouchable, outside the caste system.

Outside the casting system, we might say, in our temperate environment.

Too Much Nothingness

Use every minute, fill every gap. It's a must. Ah, how happy are they who are exempt from the anguish of idleness, the slow boil! 'Yes, happy are the contemplative ones,' dreams the Agité. Happy are those who appreciate the down time, the leisurely weekends, the aimless walks, the idle moments. Happy, but rare, beings. I have met one, maybe two, whom I did not find insupportable. All around me are only rushing, pressure, overpressure, self-inflicted pressure. As if it were always necessary to add something, to push, to live life like a compressor, a compost of refuse that is supposed to generate some kind of new shoots. Before we've finished chewing what's in our mouths, a new spoonful is coming in. With one feverish hand we stir the pot while the other hand adds seasoning. The grub that is simmering never gets cool. The fear of missing something transmutes into a terror of being useless, of being good for nothing. To be forgotten, that is the enemy! The supreme punishment: an inert telephone. Not to keep up anymore with the others is the ultimate failure.

Uselessness is a mark of infamy, a handicap, a failing. OK, quick, do something. A squirt of adrenalin, get busy with something, now! To stop would be unbearable. Then you might become lucid; and in those moments, the thought of death, intermittent as it may be, would break through. To avoid reflecting on the reasons behind our actions, we keep moving. We get bruised, we tie ourselves in knots. We over-commit; we step up the tempo. We accelerate out of fear of falling behind. The time of the appointment, its location, even the reason for it, we forget — who cares! We show up, anyway. We rush. We are always putting out fires. We don't do anything else anymore. We prove to everybody, we prove to ourselves that we can do it. And we are astonished, one day, to find ourselves exhausted, worn out for no clear reason.

Abysmal situations where the Agité no longer has time to take stock. Whole professions are marked with this syndrome. Journalist-writers, advertising executive-showmen, businessmen-athletes, model-actresses, architect-lecturers, analyst-consultants, turbo-prof-artists. . . all caught up in double employment, or triple, victims of general dissatisfaction and the fear of being sidelined. The most commonplace practices resound with it. Reading the newspaper has become reading the newspapers, skimming the press, in bulk, to get rid of it. Sucking it in while flying through it. Reading magazines with the television on, a televisual hubbub parasitized by CNN. No one is spared, and yet no one is duped; everyone knows accumulation kills; "too much information kills information," "too much tax. . .", too many activities kills activity: bicycles, mountain bikes, ATVs, bungee-jumping, rollerblades, we want to try them all.

We should take a few healthy measures. The hell with the weeklies that have been piling up for a month and that we hold onto in the vain and guilt-racking hope of reading them one day, when a break in the tumult leaves us a moment's leisure. This hiatus, this mythical moment, when we would be alone and on our own, will never come! It's this hope that gives birth to stress, as the idea that we have to be well-groomed gives rise to the nail-clipper. But no one really gets that. Males and females alike are caught up in this orgy that has us pile up people like objects, that has us mistake encumbrances for culture. The greed of the accumulators, collectors of food processors, grills, espresso-makers, all seized with convulsive passions for these knickknacks of the boom years. We pounced on the first cyclopean, greenish, boxy computers. A well-known syndrome, "technostalgia." The mind is converted, little by little, into a gigantic collection of bric-a-brac, a Salvation Army warehouse where old loves are held onto like old loaves of bread, full of stale memories, and people break up, and people deceive one another, and people have children but on the side, for we need to experience everything, to experiment, to see things both straight-on and in profile. And very often in low profile.

My Life is a Precipice

I am no exception to this rule. First of all, I have to take pen in hand, or grab my laptop, and keep up with a hurricane of deadlines; I have to let loose like a hail of bullets the torrents of my experiences, affirming, contradicting, announcing, asserting, rebuffing. I have to be agitated, knit my brows, gnash my teeth, and sit motionless, and twist my tail to stay seated. The exalted, the passionate, the intoxicated, the irritated — those who always seek the extremes — will understand me. There is something of a fundamental oxymoron in this thesis. You have to stop in order to run; to restrain yourself in order to explode; to sit down to stay the course, to achieve the breakthrough that cannot be forced. Like Jules Verne. To have to keep your feet under the table and report on tremendous storms and conflicts when one would like to be roaming the seas, piloting spacecrafts, living a life in grand style; to be the hero that you are painfully, sentence by sentence, writing into being. This torture is not new, but its hammer still cracks the best-armed brains.

No one can resist the pounding. It's not concrete under our occiputs. This is a challenge. A cliff. Whoever conquers it is, all on his own, all the guns of Navarone.

A vein, a crack, a streak in the marble, a stripe in the mother-of-pearl, those are the things that develop, that are suited to writing. I could just collapse in an armchair and smoke my pipe. Then I'd unleash my pen they way one unleashes dogs, so that it would run all over the blank page. The words would ooze out as the sap drips from the maples, filling the buckets. I can see it from here, this text, good material, stretching itself to fill in the lines. A bucolic scene that recasts my usual city office into a pastoral allegory of the return from the hunt. Sound the bugle!

In my case, there's nothing to see. Every page is a sweat.

Agités of Every Nation, Relax

Others, who do not write, are agitated just the same. They run, catch trains on the fly, buttonhole each other, monopolize, steal from each other. Streams of cocktail napkins, used-up cartridge pens, proposals, counter-proposals, the day's events. Sales reps, booksellers attacked under their piles of tomes with overheated cover designs, conquistadors of the *in-octavo*, designers, doctors, ladies' tailors, immigrant workers riveted to their Singer sewing machines, all prisoners of acceleration, subjected, body and soul, exhausted, valorous. Fear of the machine.

Are You a Shaman or an Adapter Plug?

In the great array of Agités, there are two categories. Those who keep on stretching, and those who go to pieces. The first, a sort of urban shaman, come and go at the same time. They spread, they are on the move, they relocate, travel, thrive via rhizomes. They are everywhere at once. Two cars, five jobs, three homes. The latter settle in and pick locks. Followers of Shiva, pathological octopuses with suction-cupped tentacles, they organize their raids from inside their office and their living rooms. Motionless, they extend their members like grappling hooks. They are today's pirates.

The Belgian cartoonist Franquin conceived his *Marsupilami*, another highly-strung contortionist, while watching a streetcar conductor. An Agité by any measure, the good man was passing out tickets, shifting levers, supervising maneuvers and walking through the car while giving passengers their change. He was short at least one arm. That was the tail of Marsupilami. Exasperated and imploding, bubbling over and multifaceted, Marsupilami is the Agité's mascot. Ridiculous, I admit.

No Patience to Wait? That's Normal

"A.", a "high speed" hairdresser on Sevres Street, reigns over his kingdom not only through the skill with which he wields his shears but through a psycho-astral agility for which he is famous. Unable to manage his use of time — or simply clinically maniacal — he makes appointments in such tight timeslots that by the end of the day, he is like a piston popping back and forth between chairs. He is on a mad dash from a permanent to a blow-dry, from a cut to a color, trimming and styling, and keeping up the pressure from one customer to another. It is very hard on everyone.

In the olden days, if I remember correctly (and I should, for recollections of haircuts take place so close to the brain), we used to be cradled in a dentist's chair and, the shampoo having been dealt with, the blades officiated. The better-funded chose a razor cut. There's nothing like that, today. "A" arrays his clients' skulls like so many pieces of artillery at the front, lining them up like targets to be destroyed. As a consequence of his peregrinations throughout the salon, a bad mood spreads and sometimes overflows. Of all his prisoners, I am the one who cracks first. In vain, they give me technical arguments, they explain that preparing a "square" saves precious time that will be devoted to totally transforming the appearance of a young lady who, by definition, wants to change her hairstyle while keeping it the same: that does not calm me down. In contrast to the shamanistic Agités, "A." is only at the stage of projection. He is a multiple-adapter. He inflicts on himself a gymnastic schizophrenia that exasperates everyone. He is doing everything at once, and it does not turn out badly; but everyone suffers. There is an intense feeling of being trapped and, while you clash with his reflection in the mirror (the only thing to look at except for the black hole of the magazines), you dream more and more forcefully of jumping to your feet, of bugging out of there and chopping your own hair with a piece of flint. And even of striking a fire with the flint and torching his damned hair salon.

The Agité is Compulsive, the Agité Always Wants More

Do you have any idea of what a day of ordinary agitation can be like, how many interruptions, postponements, reminders, schedule conflicts, inconveniences, changes, revisions? That is to say, ten hours carefully mapped out, by oneself; such meticulous planning. What the employee finds every day — an office, colleagues, schedules and files — the independent, whether acrobat or vagabond, has to piece together again every morning, with perseverance, assiduity, and courage.

It is already 7:00 or 8:00 AM. It's time to sit down and confine oneself to the chair, grab a pen and paper, go through the inbox, plug in a diskette. The telephone should be quiet for another two hours. Better take advantage of it, follow the game plan that Simenon suggested: write until 11:00 and then go out and gorge on the craziness of the world. For the time being, work. And now the phone rings anyway! It is an order! The first of the day. An article, a review, a commercial, an ad, a claim, a note, a plan, a sketch, scenario or screenplay... all kinds of things. The man of steel, armed with a selective anguish, for whom work means tension more than anything else, walks purposefully toward an autonomous goal, knows what to do and, especially, what not to do: he'll have to decline. The Agité, he accepts.

However, he knows that he's making a mistake, that this is how he gets himself clobbered, but his remedy is to take on more. He is a bulimic of opposites, emphatic about constraints. So he gives in to requests, adds and adds again to the workload, already suffering and already guilty about his other constraints. With a maniacal eagerness to please, he tightens the cord that strangles him. He is smothering himself in promises. He hears his own acceptance as a surrender, he slips, buries himself under the tasks to come, compresses his free time until he sees it slip away, slip out under the door, dribble down the stairs, leaving him, abandoning him to the vacuum of his excess.

Once it's rammed full like a cannon from imperial times, the use of time, the burden of Damocles, starts its mocking dance. Perched in its owner's ear, it is a stowaway that little by little becomes captain of the ship. It is *The Servant*, by Joseph Losey, at home. The plot of the kitchens. The laundry wringer.

You have to do something! Do something! Clear the area, evacuate, search, crack open the door, open the vents, the fanlight, the windows, go out on the balcony, get some air into this cubicle before it implodes and does in its owner. To write, to compose, to draft becomes a boxing match where the page is the ring and the apartment is the ropes. Anyone who lives under the office of an Agité hears him pace, paw the ground, jump up and down. It is a machine gun process, hiccups of writing, false starts, deletions; the fingers flail about on the keyboard.

The words are punches. Silence, some hot towels, the short breaks timed on a stopwatch.

Like the bullfighter, the author has his set costume. I chose, early-on, the caveman-like style of the provincial basketball coach. A soft jogging suit, with a hat in winter and a scarf wrapped twice around the throat, and sneakers. Attack garb for a literary assault. Hunched aerodynamically over the keyboard, sternum dug in, shoulders low, adopting a mountain-climber's posture for the ascent of Mount Everest, nose to the grindstone, splitting words like firewood. I give it my best. I have to! To go the distance, to keep up the pace without losing my breath or my range, as I hit the machine with a staccato burst of key-tapping. Writing is like throwing punches, uppercuts to the laptop computer. "Be funny," one says to me, "be snappy," says another, "keep it short," "can't you make it longer?" It's a weird war where every witty remark, every smart turn of phrase is a hit, almost a bullet, a shot. But I have to go help in the kitchen. Take the plates out. Everything grinds to a halt.

That is the middle ground. The only way to get started, the sole means of extracting oneself from the eternal dilemma of reconciling writing and speed, the music of words and the piercing quality of ideas. A race against the clock. Until the KO, the shower, the nightshirt. Speed is not a phenomenon but the relationship between all phenomena! In short, it is a place, *the* place, with its own laws and phenomena. You start out writing and end up on a highway. I know. I've done it. Back on the road to the Catania airport!

And then, stop. Take the time to write, that task that already appears insurmountable. The Agité has no respite and his confrontation with the computer screen is a delicate balance, like the faint glissando of the rock climber, the grumbling of the athlete with stiff muscles. If he sleeps, it is because he has crashed. If he wakes up, two hours later, opening his eyes to a night that is black as ink, he gropes around for the radio. He listens to those voices that linger on, inextinguishable, reassuring, psycho-pumps of the airwaves, plumb-lines offering a reference point in the chaos. A re-run, an interview on National Public Radio, an infusion for the half-awake synapses: "Here on *Panorama*, Nadine Vasseur welcomes. . ." The Agité never wastes a minute.

He does, however, lose. Everywhere, across the board. The universe around him extends like a battlefield, a litany of fronts on which he is retreating. Life as a whole attacks him. It is a light brigade on all sides. His education leaks out of his skull, runs out and oozes to the far horizon. Faithful to the teachings of Chairman Mao, he adheres to maxims, applies precepts. The best defense is a good offense. He charges, forges ahead, sounds the bugle, goes on the attack. He is *omnisportif*. What grows in him is not muscle but nerves. Nagged by doubt, he no longer knows whether he is reinforcing or shattering himself. On the bridge at all hours, never shirking, the Agité covers distances with great strides. How, under such conditions, can he sit still?

Office, table, chair, library, writing pad, laser-jet cartridges, printers, fax-modems! He tears around the rooms. A bourgeois occupation? You think so! In fact it is ideas that occupy him, worry him, permeate him, penetrate him, grip him and keep him in their thrall as though he was the worn out clutch in a lousy transmission. The only glory is in the imagination of the onlookers. Looks of envy, of desire, from all the others, the out-of-commission, the out-of-circulation, the horde.

So that is how I get down to work, by hitting the brakes; that is how the Agité takes the time to say everything, at least, amidst the metallic vibrations of the fuselages that shake under deceleration, in the ruddy glow of the brake disks, in the brazier that glows and already consumes it. Ashes and diamonds.

We Demand a Special Effort on the Part of Science

What we need: database management in the brain, with dynamic indexing. You think, and it takes notes! Whatever crackles in the half-light of the deserted office is recorded remotely. Nothing is lost. Everything is saved, the system is impeccable! Another, more antiquated method, is like a salad strainer. Dry your ideas. All the words, all the thoughts, everything that you noted in black and white in your hectic life, in your helter-skelter way, on scraps of paper or re-used floppy disks, is tossed in a bag. Then the latch, a turn of the key and presto! elbow grease! Shake it hard. It takes vigor to produce a sparkling text. For this experiment, you have to get your hand on some strong cranks, or you'll strain your tendons. Mix the ingredients well, and in just two shakes of a lamb's tail — delicately, gently — unmold it. You open the case, pull out the text. Already formatted. And it's a bestseller.

The Agité is Always Ready

I am of those guys that people call at the last minute. Not as a last resort but in an emergency. A kind of paramedic of freelance writing and sometimes even of publishing. A fireman. When they realize, at closing time, when they're putting it to bed, that they don't have a block of text to underscore the impact of a captivating "visual," they call me or one of my peers. I do not think we are so numerous. At best, a small troop of mercenaries. The last nine times out of ten, I had to deliver my prose on a rush basis. It shows in the rates charged, and in the nerves, too. Over the long run, it's like an erosion of the plumbing. The valves seize up, the bearings deteriorate and become rough.

We all agreed, last time, that after such an experience any reasonable person would refuse the next such assignment, and especially as it would have to be superimposed onto an already full schedule; but we Agités, under pressure, always say yes. It wears us down, wears us out; but we have to take up the challenge, be present, never be missing. For my part, a part that I know is widely shared, I take it as an opportunity to achieve a small physical exploit, to win out over the beast, to deny my fatigue, to reinvigorate myself with the blizzard that insults my use of time. These productions to countdown, they are my personal Annapurnas. Any serious Agité, however, knows that a good book, written from start to finish, would bring him real success, more than this whole armada of odd jobs, and a more authentic income than split royalties; that a single occupation would enable him to bring the game to a close, to ignore the phone calls, to spit on the fax machine, to scold the bores and to get rid of the nuisances; in short, he could work with his personal Pantheon, without distraction; but no, we accept the odd jobs. In a moment of excited weakness, I allow myself to be corrupted. The bait of additional income and a strong desire to please, and to please myself — me that they came to ask, me that they want, that they tease the way you would poke a deer to make her bleat and jump around, I say yes, finding in this additional work a good reason to interrupt what I have already achieved through pain and suffering. I offer myself a break, to some extent. I assassinate myself.

There is no doubt that, adept as we are at fleeing straight ahead, we are actually handicapped when it comes to turning people down. No doubt at all. Fear of lack? Yes. Fear of lacking orders, of lacking confidence, of lacking talent. Fear of being pathetic. Like good drug addicts, it is in this state of lack that one calms down, in a suicidal workaholic excitation. And not one among us will have time, in the end, to pen his own "obit," his parting self-definition, squeezed tight as a fist, an express formula: "Died. Too soon."

Is this reasonable?

My Office

So we talk, we chat, we gab. Make noise, at least. A hub-bub pierced with strident cadences and bursts of laughter. A parabolic, hyperbolic agitation that transforms our little four-some into a pizzeria by the train station, a bureaucratic market-place. One guy is handing another a pile of photocopies over my shoulder, and while I torture myself trying to stick my ear right through the telephone to find out who has called me, she twitters on and on about the umpteenth preview or gives her opinion on "the press that has sold out" and various pseudo-trends. The door slams, regurgitating a batch of messengers, parcels, packages, all of yesterday's shopping.

Any and all of them could, in fact, avoid my little junkyard and, after many pretended feints and scuffles, allow themselves to sink, a little further down the hall, into a wobbly armchair. But the armchairs are annoying, they feel like garbage bags tossed into the back of your knees, and no one has the strength to face such a row of massive hulks. And no one aspires to it, for as we all like to say, inspiration lies in all this boiling, seething interaction. The agitated multitude that keeps on telescoping. How many times did your door open and close again, how many colleagues came bounding in, for no reason at all, or just for a word, to ask a question, to hear a good joke? Reflection is cut short, debates are curtailed, all for the excitement of urgency. And everyone shouts to all the others; they yell and interrupt each other.

And we call that life at the office.

Elsewhere, the guy who is waving his arm around in his BMW sweeps the air with his arm and bumps the rear view mirror; he is a member of the "hands free" club. Right in the middle of Columbus Circle, he's making a phone call. And this other guy who seems serious, almost dormant, telephone in his right hand, left hand under his chin, is exasperated as soon as you say hello. He was listening to his messages! And because of you, he didn't hear anything! Now he has to play back the message again! But here's the problem: while we're all good at "deleting," destroying, getting rid of messages that we don't want, we are not too good at figuring out the play-back keys. To "listen to a message again," do you press "5" and "#," or "*5*"? Who knows?

It's an absolute rule that every conversation is interrupted by a phone call. And not only calls that one receives but even calls that one cannot keep oneself from making. As if the hands were acting on their own, flicking adroitly across the number pads, landing us in the stratosphere of answering machines and answering services that pass by each other on the sea of messages, in a big-bang of uncontrolled electronic pulses. People don't even take responsibility for their answering machines anymore.

Nobody takes responsibility for anything, anymore. Today, Boris Vian would write: "I will crash on your tombs." He wouldn't have to come up with a pseudonym, he would sign with his cyberzip and humanity, caught up in a morbid acceleration, at the end of the race would hit the wall at the end of the train line.

In this era of propulsion, of rushing, Agités are giddy with the speed attained in the total absence of protection. No windshield, no seatbelts. We just dash ahead. The goal doesn't matter anymore. No time. Change is all around us. Too much intensity, too much distressing density.

For fear of not maintaining our distance, we don't stay in place anymore. Instead of putting down roots, we rack up mileage and the landscape ends up unraveling so quickly that it melts little by little into a spongiform magma with neon highlights.

Better than all the biomorphisms, the synthesized images, virtual twists, better than any commentary, Merleau-Ponty dubs it "the shooting star of confusion."

From Agitation to Confusion

Accumulation does not happen without generating some confusion. In his *Alphabet*, Gilles Deleuze talks about Plato, creating the concept of pure idea — something that would be only itself and nothing else — a mother who would be only mother, although we know that a mother is also a woman and the daughter of another mother. Concepts are created, points out Deleuze, that respond to needs. Pure idea, in disregarding any other consideration, made it possible to sort out the applicants to the government of Athens. They needed a way to organize their claims on a hierarchical basis, to judge them only on their capacity to serve as chief, the "shepherd of men." Pure idea is a means of selection.

Today, the concept of pure idea is in decay. No longer pure, it is putrefying, and now obstructs all the decision-making processes. There's no more question of choosing and thus of giving an opinion, no more question of governing. The philosophies of de-responsibilization (psychoanalysis, Marxism, etc.) have re-shuffled the deck. Weak democracy is the rule. "Anything goes," but nothing is going anywhere. Nobody is really playing anymore. The debate is closed beforehand. Consensus is a panacea that leads to resignation. Nobody takes a position anymore or, rather, we accept all positions. We are everywhere and nowhere, and we dissolve in this effervescence, a catalepsy of hiccups, squirming like pug dogs. We bark, but everything goes on just the same. Enslavement to "whatever." Of all the qualities that make up agitation, we retain only the "simultaneity" that allows us to be everything at once, one thing and the other and its opposite. Not to be.

Carole Bouquet and Klaus Barbie

Thanks to the manipulation of virtual images, Jean Gabin

will soon be playing in movies that he did not have time to film while he was alive. And so, we will come to doubt his death (unless, a still more tragic effect, we come to doubt our own reality). Will we be, tomorrow, both dead and alive at the same time? Certain variety shows are edifying on this point. By a subtle assembly of interviews, they already give the impression that a star who has disappeared (and who is not missed) is still among us. During a retrospective on Claude Francois, the late actor appeared to be answering questions. How docile are the archives! This confusion is magnified in the trailer of Claude Berri's distressing film *Lucie Aubrac*. Scrolling up over a background of clichéd images (a train derailment, unshaven Resistance fighters, old wrecks on the riverside quays), the names of the leading actors appear: Carole Bouquet, Daniel Auteuil and then suddenly Jean Moulin, Klaus Barbie! But it's the actors impersonating them who appeared on screen, such as Patrice Chéreau, in the envied role as the leader of the Resistance (decked out for the occasion with a comical white scarf as a socialist candidate at the town hall of Gardanne), but no, it is Barbie's name that is given. A generic Barbie. Casting above all. Here, thus, hired for the occasion, are Daniel Auteuil and Jean Moulin. The re-publication of Lucie Aubrac's book, *Ils partiront en ivresse*, adds a little hook. To attract readers, the editor inserted a group of photographs in the middle of the book. These are stereotypes from Berri's films, not from the era itself: Carole Bouquet in a Lyon street, with the caption, "Lucie Aubrac goes to the Kommandant." It's too bad for our students. Codes are offended, logic is demolished, and socio-logic is destroyed. The floodgates are open, the tidal wave is beyond control. And when a French rapper, Doc Gyneco, spit out some nonsense with strong anti-Semitic tonalities ("the yids explode and open the stores"), the director of Virgin France (Emmanuel de Burtel) took up his defense in *Libération* in the name of "the way kids talk" and "in defense of the rappers" who, as every one knows since the NTM and Toulon incidents, are victims of Fascism. Go ahead, kids, let it roll.

In the Objective: the Negative

Accumulation is a routine obligation today. For the screenplay writer, intensifying the profundity is a substitute for the quasi-disappearance of boundaries. Thus, in recent years, films have been keen on using the long-distance lens. By crushing the image, they add density and give it more grain. This is not just the result of an aesthetic preference, but the over-exploitation of filming capabilities, induced by the proliferation of technical accessories.

Producers used to work without a monitor. They shot a reel and stood by the results. The invention of talking movies was accompanied by a diversification of film standards. Other technical innovations further modified the traditional assumptions of cinematography. The appearance of the "scope" format, then the 70mm, created havoc in re-distributing films. Local movie houses would show imposing epics that were shamefully shorn. Victor Mature, a famous fighter, found himself systematically beheaded as soon as he appeared in America, leaving nothing more on the screen but the explosion of his pectorals crowned by a hint of a jaw. As the years passed, technical progress only made the situation worse. Today, scenario writers make their films "at the same time" for the large and the small screen, for the cinema and television. Rather than going back and forth between one and the other, they rely on their picture monitor. Different frames show, in dotted lines (small for TV, larger for the cinema). Going from film to TV inescapably involves losing the sides of the image. What is registered on the film, to the left and the right, is lost, "projected" into limbo. Our eye may be accustomed to compensating for this loss of image if, say, in a Sergio Leone scene, a screen saturated with desert suggests to us that Clint Eastwood must be hiding somewhere off to the right of the TV, between the window and the CD-player; but our eye is unable to locate the same peculiarities when they happen vertically. Moreover, while the TV cuts the film in width, it stretches it by 20% in height! To counter these effects, to adapt all standards, to calibrate the various types of films. . . they re-shoot, they transfer, they subject the film to a thousand technical tortures. It's no use saying that the frame, which yesterday required all the talent of a great director, is nothing any more but a memory.

To prove that, let's go to the movies. What's being shown

there only very rarely maintains the integrity of the border of the frame. It is blurry, indistinct, dispensable. It takes courage and tenacity to film, as Scorsese still does in *Casino*, a Robert De Niro penetrating the frame on the far right, against a panoramic background; on TV, the actor will have only the viewers' imagination to count on, if he is not to have exited from the scene entirely.

The loss of the frame, the disappearance of panoramic perspectives: these two elements are combined in the use of long focal distances. While crushing the image, as the telephoto lens does, these focal distances make it richer. But it is an enrichment that coarsens the image. The frame is fuzzy, the image is heavy. In a world stripped of any geometrical reference mark, this double phenomenon suits the image of our universe, increasingly dense and less and less precise. Thus, like an Agité's filofax, over-committed on every page with a confusion of appointments — postponed, crossed out, moved to a different location — the cinema reflects a reality that piles things up and slides off in every direction. A world that is drained. A jungle, you would think; but in reality, the Sahel. A dark Sahel.

Visuals and Puff Pastry

Because computer information is multi-layered like a napoleon, because with hypertext one click on an icon and a new world spews forth, one would hope that the symbols of a bygone era would adjust to take account of these new circumstances. Then you could refresh when you get overloaded. The smallest e-zine is a visual deluge, a graphic overdose. The titles, the designs and layouts overlap, abuse, catapult and murder each other. One web page cannibalizes another.[3]

Everything is an overload. The reader, threatened, feels tempted at the end of a few pages to shout, stop! Stop the website! I want to get out. So, to counter the nausea, fanatics have established their own techniques for maintaining their distance, the techniques of an Agité: they make a point of never *reading* a cyber-magazine, they just surf from one to another; and they always do something else at the same time, tapping a keyboard, handling a remote control. They overload to escape superabundance, they accelerate to avoid seeing all the obstacles, they melt the universe into a magma in which all asperities are leveled. They prefer the indistinct over the flat, and not the already-been-chewed anymore but vomit.

"The Comrades Disperse but Remain Active" (A Saying from the Sixties)

You can tell at first glance that that guy is not OK. A waxen complexion, circles under the eye, an unhealthy diet, and about 50 pounds over what he weighed last year. His baggy clothes don't hide anything, everything is overflowing and his thin hair is evidence of a collapse. However, that guy has resources. He is active, a mover of ideas. With his sneakers, he pounds the pavement, he puts his shoulder to the wheel, he moves monuments. With an anxious gaze, and a cascade of ideas all tangled together; the words are smashing into each other in their rush to come out of his mouth.. For twenty years, H. has regularly taken *Survector* every morning, a drug like Prozac, an "upper," as he says. The name is already a propellant, and the explanation he gives is more exciting still. "Every morning, I wake up so full of ideas that *Survector* helps keep me together." *Together!*[4] Ubique et orbi. He would be laughable, if one did not guess that behind this desire for control lay an attempt to fight the instincts for mastery, and an anguish over the dispersion that echoes shamanistic passions. Those of the wise Siberian who, scattered by lightning to the four corners of the Yakut tundra, awakes reconstituted. And endowed with a super-ability to see everything and everywhere. He is *together* and *everywhere*. The one who is pulverized by God has an advantage over those who self-destruct: primal experience. The city-dweller, stuffed with prescription drugs, has not passed the test that initiates the shaman, and so he elevates him to the divine level. The *Survector*-ized (a little like vasectomized), is a psychically castrated being who is reconstituted every morning. *Survector* is the prosthesis and, without it, he is liable to burst. Thus his attitude is a case in point. The anguish of having too much to say is clotted in the sad fact that there is not enough time to say it. A time famine, the scissors effect on a diminished timeframe when has too much living to do. So, yes, H. is trying to pull himself together, to do on his own what other people do via team sports, a good scuffle in the scrum. And so one can see how much the Agité is a recluse thrown into the challenge to become a group, all on his own. He fills his loneliness through a federative schizophrenia that he keeps under control. He keeps piecing his multiple and fractured identity back together the way fractures are mended, by compression. He compresses himself the way a fracture heals itself.

Techno

Let's go, full speed ahead, attack! To the point of complete exhaustion. Fight! Follow the trail, delude ourselves, consume ourselves. In 1995, I went out with the photographer Xavier C; we took a deep breath and plunged into the world of London's techno clubs. For eight nights we went searching for the "biggest sound," with the bass echoing in our sternums and our myocardia; eight nights in a row, visiting cesspools of chaos, to arrive at a state of constant tremors and severe cotton-mouth every morning, with the be-bop of my toothbrush awakening the rhythmic staccato and the aggressive punch of *house music*.

When the least echo of a jackhammer inflates your chest with a delirious excitement, it is clearly time to sound the alarm. Only here, in an environment where the clamor of every siren is an essential component of the décor, what is left that can serve as a warning?

The slippery slope. From extreme agitation to exaltation and from exaltation to vertigo. For in abandoning oneself to the electronic din (or, yesterday, to LSD), or even to hallucinatory, revolutionary *agitprop*, it is the same anorexia that is at work. It digs its tunnels and hollows out reality, looking to substitute an infinite vacuum for the world that rejects us or escapes us. In this sense, this vast blinding splash is not the promising sign of exaltation but exhaustion. And certainly, our long, pale faces, the hollows carved under our burning eyes, our sick coughs were well all there to prove, how clearly!, that a full week of sound bombardment, inflated with ecstasy, with soft-drinks and with the sweaty convulsions of the dance floor, was heading us straight to the knockout.

Anger, agitation, gesticulation are not ways of gaining control but of abandoning it, they are projections without limits. Trying to go beyond the limits is a prison, extending this "no exit" situation *ad infinitum*, to a series of dead ends. Abandonment is a willed defeat, a resignation in which we fully participate. In the strobe-lit cavern of "United-Kingdom," stuffed with thousands of people, we spied through the vaults of cigarette smoke the tacky and suspicious-looking curtain masking the entrance to the last room. There, in the vibration of the metallic beat of music from a steel mill, we underwentwe underwent, an "extreme experience." It is a physical pleasure that must approach what rocks feel on their way into the crusher. You come out of there granulated. A perverse, ersatz, counterfeit sense of exaltation, there are so many ways to give in to this ultra-violence that is no longer rage but subservience. If the maximum physical effort, the disheveled audacity, aims to call forth energy and innovation, to break a record as one breaks his body,

there is certainly a will for control, an élan that consists in pushing to the end and to the goal: final exhaustion. A race to the
abyss under the lasers, bathed in a depressive tempo, squeezed
like a sponge, assaulted by canned music, contracting a canned
spongiform disease that destroys your hearing.

Nonetheless, I still have a secret thing for techno. It's not
easy to share, not easy to admit. I must be young and foolish.
For years, I wondered how the punks with 8-inch high Mohawk
hairdos made a living. What kind of work could they do? They
couldn't be bike messengers, since you can't install a helmet over
such a construction, right? But that's a non-issue, the wrong
question. These people do not work. They are in a stupor.[5]

Agitation in Vain

Dens of iniquity, of depravity, flashy façades where modernity is hybridized with the vulgar, in back-alleys and basements,
everywhere the tidal wave of aversion. It's hard to be a man of
one's time without blushing.

Just as there was a time when the electric fireplace log was
a must for any cozy living room, when to be "design" it had to be
Regency, there are places where Agitation is only a pale copy of
what it should be. Some restaurants have made a specialty of
that fake ambiance that clashes like sausages in a noodle dish.
The Hard Rock Café, for one. Do you know, hearty diners, that
when the cook announces to the waiter that a hamburger has
been slapped on a salad and is ready to be delivered, he doesn't

use the traditional "ready!" or even "hot!" but . . . "Rock'n'roll!"? It's pitiful, to the point of obscuring the insipid taste of the conglomeration drowned under the fries. Is that the point?

It's true that this gin mill, where the decibels are cranked up to the max for a clientele that is already intoxicated by the volume of their walkmans, has chosen for its motto the inane phrase *Serve all, love all,* as though this grease factory were a humanitarian outpost.

In these brutal sites, Pizza Pino, tapas bars, the Coupole de Montparnasse and even Mezzo Mezzo in the heart of London, Vladimir Jankélévitch's comment is apt: "Silence is a conquest of man." You can see that between the cry of the wild beasts in the savanna and the tantalizing but infernal *pizzicati* of the bad juke-box pouring into the inner rooms the pangs of pop music, there is more than a similarity, there is a resurgence. The state of nature is not found amidst the geysers of Yellowstone, the bayous of Louisiana, or the game parks of Africa, but in the shopping malls, the parking lots and the elevators where the constant drone of muzak, pierced by insipid versions of the "top 50," is the sinusoidal echo of the cruelty of the jungle.

The Hard Rock Café has many fierce competitors. At Planet Hollywood, the Model Café, the All-Stars Café, the Harley Davidson Café — they all boast maxims like: *Ride to live, live to ride.* It is true that, to some people, the roar of a Harley engine is "better than Mozart." This era of sterile Agitation bludgeons us, not so much by zapping as by repetition. The *dik-*

tat of the remote control has become an end more than a means. The medium is the message. An old tune. Getting used to chaos, self-service Parkinson's, is a downfall. A few years ago Jean-Marc Parisis published a book called *The Melancholy of Fast Food*. That says it all. Fake Agitation, a real distress.

By trying to grab too much, the Agité is likely to lose his grip. He who embraces too much has a poor grasp. Haunted by a crawling cockroach, repelled by the horror of an inexpressive but thundering world, he has to prove his interests. To justify his racing quest. Or suffer the contempt of everyone who is "above that."

Do it Again, Do it Again, Set Another Record

The sources of rivers have been reached, explored, drained; frontiers pushed back, jungles destroyed, forests exfoliated and, worse still, sexuality voided of passion. Pressed like grapes, grated like a carrot, such is our planet in the era of disappearances. The conquest is complete. Agités, incapable of restraining their desire to pursue the quest, in spite of everything — fugitives no longer heading for a goal but absolutely dedicated to eradicating their anguish — slowly sink in the effort to escape depression. They get all worked up, all for nothing.

A veil that masks everything, distorts everything. Equalizing and crushing under the cover of promotion. Exploits are in fashion; conquests are forgotten. *The Guinness Book of Records*, itself a record-breaking bestseller, inventories them in a confusion that mixes the voluntary overachievement with tragic accidents. In a compulsive fascination for lists, theories and collections of names are grouped randomly under headings like the names on a petition, so that a hunger striker finds himself next to someone who underwent an involuntary fast when the police forgot him in a cell. Asceticism, once a form of contemplative introspection, a solitary period of being with one's self like the "days of silence" that Henri Michaux used to reserve for himself, is now classified as an attempt to break a record. What's "never been done" becomes the "never been seen." How snide is the expression "pointless achievements."[6] Franz Kafka saw it coming, he who wrote a novella entitled "A Champion of Fasting." Asceticism has evolved into a meaningless record, devoid of real value. Since then, even contemplation has lost its place. It has been reduced to just one particular phase of agitation. What distinguished it yesterday has been leveled, today.[7] The equal sign that tyrannizes, levels, flattens, destroys all differences and prohibits comparisons, should be associated with the sloppy repetition of "more and more" that ends up wearing us out. Quantity over quality. Then asceticism really begins. It's the first stage of an exaltation that finds further stimulation in deprivation. The toxins of fatigue, the lack of sleep re-injected into the body, push us to the end. The narcosis that grips the marathon-runner. There's none of that sobriety at the heart of intoxication that is, indeed, the real sign of intoxication. In *The Hunger*, the character of Knut Hamsun chooses famine as much as he is subjected to it. It intoxicates him, stimulates him to the point of vomiting. A practical ritual, the magic of adversity, of the impossible. Proximity of muscular and nervous collapse. The trance of rejection.

Pessimism.

An example. The *South China Morning Post* announces that Paul McCartney has launched a chat program on the Internet. A global interview. What an initiative. Only, it soon becomes clear that, given the tumultuous flood of connections, he will not be able to answer them all. At one minute per question, it would take at least ten years to satisfy everyone. The *new-look* initiative turns into a farce and the legendary Beatle has to resort to the dullest sort of press conference. His producer finally reveals to the journalists the goal of the entire operation: to make Paul McCartney the most-interviewed man in the world, in order to place him, once more, in the great *Book of Records.*

How disappointing, what an unimaginably stupid waste of time. But also what a lesson! What a way to summarize an entire era in which only impulses count. Quantity. The all-powerful seismograph. A stiletto rather than a stylus. A point without the diamond.

Misty memories of Jean-Michel Jarre's "Docks Concert" in London. In an uninterrupted barrage of sound, three hours long, with a powerful light show bouncing off all the nearby buildings and a Hollywood-like fireworks display that destroyed any scenario, any melody, any magic of the explosions in the frozen silence. They one-upped the supermarkets in providing too much of everything. Music, light-show, drum machines, again: "quantity over quality." A hash, a disturbing mayhem later reconstructed in the studio. The band, the central feature, the great lie that would make everyone who couldn't be there think that they had missed a big event — the concert of the century. A trick, like the "marginal general public," the category in which this French techno-star's producer classifies him.

– The Cannes Film Festival?

– A crowd of professionals elbowing each other in front of the Palace of Festivals, looking for a trash can so they can dump the press kits.

Dostoyevsky of the Poor

So, disgust the ascendancy of the material, dash outside and look for the real world. Go see how it is someplace else. There's always a chance that you'll find something. You want to get away from yourself but he comes along; there's nothing to do, the problem is within us. The planetary Agité, an exalted traveler, is always an idiot. He is like Dostoyevsky's Prince Muishkin, on a mission that he will end up failing. He is making good progress. And then an incident occurs. He who was hurrying to the train for Moscow, urged by the pressing goal of preventing a misalliance, a marriage, a tragedy, here he goes and starts a quarrel in a tavern, then stops in shock at the sight of a dead cat flattened by a trolley car, then meets a friend and from there is inveigled into stopping for tea. And suddenly, "Good heavens! my train!" He throws his jacket over his shoulders and, without another word, runs down the sidewalk toward the station whose lights have long since gone out and whose doors are locked tight. That's how it is for the Agités. We follow a long course toward some discovery, when a chance meeting distracts us. And so we stray farther from our goal, and also from our starting place. We get lost, and our behavior, frantic but changeable, inept and volatile, is exasperating. He who was so firmly decided now cruelly appears lost, irresolute, wandering, weak-willed. Like the Idiot who, caught in a burning building with the crowd shouting at him to come out, while the flames attack the walls, runs from one floor to another, choking in the smoke, and dithering. He shuffles his feet. "Come on, get out of there!" howl his friends and strangers from the sidewalk. And he, hesitant, suddenly so weary, so distant, almost feverish in the furnace that is climbing the stairs: "Yes, yes, of course, but before I do, I need to find the answer to a question. . . which, unfortunately, I have forgotten." And there he is, racking his brain to find the approximate terms while the floors crash down and the stairways, too. Out in the street, shivering in their overcoats, freezing in the snow, stamping from one foot to the other, jostled by the firemen, the fascinated onlookers shout in unanimous horror: "What an idiot!" while this scatterbrain is burning in hell. Deleuze[8] understood why the noble Russian, quickly driven out of the new society, liquidated by the revolution, found his most trusty servant in Kurosawa. The noble Russian on the verge of extinction and the Samurai whose entire philosophy would soon run up against the cruel reality of the firearm were facing the same renunciation, the same swallowing up. The same passion, soon blocked forever by the uselessness of both the Samurai and the nobleman, unite the two in the same chaotic, frenetic rhythm, carried away and de-railing. The Agité is always in conflict that way, aware of the immense vacuity of his vociferations, sweaty and rushed, and propelled nonetheless by the hope that masterpieces may sometimes be born from disasters.

Reporters

The cameraman and soundman are a hellish couple that lately tends to be fused together. Yesterday, they were agitated together, crawling between charred vehicles, running from an entryway to the corner of a wall, climbing the rubble, going down hallways. A waltz of the opposites. The cameraman, focused on his target, is oblivious to everything that is out of his range. With his sherpa to look after him. The soundman, whose ears explode with every leaf that is stepped on, whose tympanums are assaulted by the crunching of gravel, the slamming of doors, by muffled cries and gunshots, has to shove to the right, pull to the left, guide along a wall, push to the ground his cyclops of a companion. It's the speed of sound against that of matter. While a shot may be heard before it lands, the respite is brief. It is lightning-quick. In that interval, while remaining riveted to the microphone, he has to summon the physical strength to yank his fellow-professional from the panoramic view. Sight and hearing yield the command to dorsal flexibility, to fleetness of foot. To contemplate, to capture an image, is to fix the eye while the body is in a trance. Impulse in fission.

The soundman and his cameraman, holed up in their hotel room, are the modern-day equivalents of that congenital idiot. The wanderers who thought they were conquerors suddenly find out they are runaways, traitors to their land, their friends and families. What were they looking for, in setting out for the wild blue yonder, risking their lives on the front lines? Once the desire to traverse the world has evaporated, the urge to get closer to the flame, what is left to keep them from heading home? The floor is mildewed, there's dust. It's lonely. "Here we are in Dacca, surrounded, waiting for the final assault."[9] And suddenly reality hits like a thunderbolt. And Bruce Chatwin's question, which we have all had on our lips at some point and which haunts us still: "What the hell am I doing here?"[10]

Heartbreak Hotel

The instinct for mastery has taken over the whole planet. Because the Agité is a traveler, because he is full of pep, because he'll walk over hot coals, he sees the ground slipping away beneath his feet. He finds it, then it eludes him. It deceives him. Travel, distance, melancholy. In the hotel room he is suddenly depressed. So far from everything and everyone. Given up in suffering. Where is all that exaltation that had buoyed us along so far? It's disappeared, flown away. When the alarm clock wakes us, we are orphaned by all that had drawn us on so passionately. Now it all seems senseless. We're disorientated. There's an inversion at work. We wanted to disappear, and here we are being held, being pulled back. The elastic syndrome. The farther afield one goes, the harder it is stretched. Backlash! And a state of shock. Groggy with loneliness, asleep on one's feet, KO'd. As soon as we head out, aren't we already on the way back? What's the difference?

"The ambiguity of travel —" writes Nicolas Bouvier, "— you become attached, you tear yourself away, and this pendulum-like motion is not at all anodyne. You swing from jubilation to sadness, and this oscillation, which is like a trip within the trip, kills you."[11] It's a baroque, or *barroco*, position: the Hispano-Portuguese word was first used in 1531 to indicate a particularly brilliant pearl. An abnormality, a journey, a shift. The exaltation of the mystical paintings of Zurbaran, the double motion of the Prague baroque, the contortion of the sculptures of Mathias Bernard Braun, the painful compactness of Ferdinand Maximilian Brokof's characters, the immobile distresses of statues, always swinging between the crash and the ascendance, elevation and nightmare. A melancholic process reactivated at every new departure.

In 1543, the word adventurer still meant something. To Rabelais, it signified a "man of war, a mercenary." I would have a hard time, today, to say what is the just cause for which the Agité fights, in airports and in motels. During a duel to the death, an Englishman taunted the Frenchman Surcouf, saying, "We fight for honor, you fight for money." Surcouf stung him in reply, "Everyone fights for that which he lacks." This is not the time, alas, to relate his response. We today subscribe, rather, to a war of nerves, hope and endurance. As Pascal Quignard wrote, quoting Fronton's *Principia Historiae* — but it also applies to the agitation of ideas, the network, the inclination to cite a citer's citation — "Wandering across the globe, there is no goal to their voyages. They travel, not to make it to some place, but to an evening."

However, we traverse conflicts like so many deserts or trenches pocked with shrapnel: offices that are vales of tears, rental car agencies, the hotel check-in, savings banks, waiting rooms, foreign exchange offices, room-services, taxis, rickshaws, trains and planes delayed or cancelled; customs circumvented, papers counterfeited, the mystique of meetings that mutate into throbbing wanderings. . . wars that we support. The eternal return of the same. And to yourself.

The Ritual of the Voyage

So we set out, nevertheless. Snap shut your suitcase, check your passport, your papers, your dollars. Hesitate, take a few things out, lighten the bags. By your thousandth trip, you don't worry that much about packing. You can usually find anything you need when you get there. The basics. Only where sanitary care is deficient, you have to take care of yourself. Cleaning your lenses with water from a gutter can ruin your eyes. Buying soap, toothpaste, shampoo, is a two-mile exploit from Kuching, in northern Borneo, and a gamble in rural Corsica, not to mention Kalmykia. While the combatant may go without brushing his teeth for fifteen days in a lifetime, it is harder to withstand the cold for fifteen hours in a row in a *krushchëvba*, those hollow brick buildings tossed together in the storm of the 1960's to placate the *muzhiks*. Thirty years later, these dilapidated buildings are still, I hesitate to claim, standing. They creak under the snow, smelly and sinister in the soot and the emanations of cabbage. Trip after trip, that is what one thinks about: the discomfort. Then, someone twists your arm. You cover yourself with amulets, anoint yourself as the ancients did. A voyage has its magic rituals. At every milestone, we have our hooks to keep ourselves attached to the edge of the world, and in moments of terrible desolation, to recall some memory of salvation. You don't have to adore high-heel shoes, garters, or hunting knives to be a fetishist. The traveler has his charms, a pleasing blend of pretense and sorcery, a disguise for the open highway, an operetta-like protection suitable for voyages, a pleasant psychic colonization and cruel coercion.[12] Whatever route you choose, you always run the risk of ending up at some godforsaken, desolate, nameless way-station, a misty siding where the shape of life in a cul-de-sac, futile and humiliating, is all that is offered. Spleen, distress, no gas. Nostalgia.[13]

Some co-opt the problem, giving a pet name to the break-down. They cherish it, caress it, they start to like even the depressing wallpaper of their boarding house. They sink into alcohol and polish off one bottle after another, faster than a whole group of people would do. It is boredom that eats them. A dull gaze, slipping over the landscape. A street in Sichuan, the *100,000 Lilies* conglomerate of building sites in central Peking, a distressing primitiveness; Malecon de Saint-Domingue whipped by a nasty wind on a murky, ominous sea of swells; calamitous trees, the dry dust of a 1960's hotel in the outskirts of Niamey, in Nigeria; a film of ice on the bathroom mirror in a hotel with no customers, no heat, and no future, somewhere in Kirdjeli, in the icy mountains of a remote Bulgarian province where electricity has not yet made its way... The habitué still finds a compelling poetry, an irresistible appeal in the enumeration of these exotic places. This is not vanity but a game the mind plays. Bugs in the memory.

Around the World in 80 Duty-Free Shops

Memory, and souvenirs. If it goes on this way, persistent travelers (those who have not yet admitted the futility of any physical displacement) will no longer have the pleasure of devoting themselves to the notorious nonsense that, for the affluent, consisted in traveling the world from one duty-free shop to the next. With luck, they can pick up here something to put in the box they picked up there. Soon, given the rate of supranational alliances, with trade barriers falling like a house of cards, there will be no use in looking to buy things at reduced prices, when they are in any case already obsolete. Frankly, what's the point of taking photographs anymore? Alain Finkielkraut gave Paul Virilio the tourist's eschatology of an entire world given up to the entertainment of the masses.[14] A dismal perspective of a universe destroyed by the *ersatz* of what was, yesterday, exploration. In the words of Hannah Arendt (what better way to evoke Finkielkraut than by quoting Arendt?), "There is no mass culture, there are only the leisure pursuits of the masses, which are attacking culture;" then, yes, the car is the avant-garde of the horde, the precursory sign of a global victory of the squadrons of imbeciles. However, demonizing the tourist did not begin yesterday. From time immemorial, the holiday-maker has been the subject of farce,[15] immortalized in his tee-shirt ("San Francisco," "Bangkok," and "University of Paris" [in English] — the most enigmatic), with his hairy legs sticking out, his sun hat, and his video camera bouncing on a beer-belly. Even so, he is gaining ground. During an episode in his series *Replies* on the France Culture channel, Finkielkraut evoked the distressing future of a world where tourists won't find anything but more tourists. The Piazza San Marco in Venice and the piers of Chicago are the early reflections of this trend, heralding a great leveling accom-

plished by the wearing of shorts. Then, yes, we will commemo-
rate and venerate, as a blessed time that is long gone, the 1970's
and 1980's where we would crowd like a flock of sheep into a
duty-free shop in order to take home some local specialty (most
often made in Japan) at discount prices. Thus was forgotten the
intention of walking out to meet the locals, the other. Only the
centrifugal egocentric imperialism, "the projection of one's own
subjectivity."[16]

The Agité enamored of time zones and baggage carts, skipping over the globe, proud of all his visas and stamps the way
others show off their military decorations, is an endangered species.

On my refrigerator I have a magnet, a drawing by Hergé.
Tintin perched on a motorbike. Burning rubber, he shouts to his
trusty dog:

"We're making headway!"

That's it. We're making headway.

But toward what?

Footnotes

1. Russell Miller, *Bunny, the Real Story of "Playboy,"* translated into French under the title *L'Histoire excessive de "Playboy,"* Albin Michel, 1987.

2. "Only the weight never wears out." (Emmanuel Levinas).

3. See Mark Dery, *Vitesse virtuelle. La cyberculture aujourd'hui*, Abbeville Press, 1997.

4. Together; or, if you're working on your French accent, "two-*gaser*" — making it a double chemical propulsion, if such a thing exists.

5. "If one doesn't manipulate things and try to make them conform to one's will, one gives in to their inertial force and follows them wherever they flow." (Roger Caillois, *Instinct et Societes*, Gonthier, p. 52.)

6. On this subject, see the excellent No. 61 of the review *Communications* (Seuil, 1996) and in particular the article "Le Corps acteur et le corps agi," by Jacques Cloarec.

7. In *Communications, op. cit.*, see Pierre Pachet's article, "La privation volontaire," p. 93.

8. Speaking at a conference at FEMIS.

9. "Dacca is surrounded, and we are waiting for the final attack," an article by Pierre Bois, international reporter for *Le Figaro*, published in 1972, in *Grand reportages, 43 prix Albert-London*, Points Actuels, p. 411.

10. Bruce Chatwin, *Qu'est-ce que je fais là*, Grasset.

11. Nicolas Bouvier, *L'Echappée belle, éloge de quelque pèlerins*, Métropolis, p. 38-39.

12. Belgian colonialism was once known as "jovial coercion," as opposed to the French colonialism that was considered "rough paternalism."

13. It was an Alsatian doctor, Andréas Hofer, who coined the word "nostalgia" from *nostos* (return) and *algia* (pain), to describe the state of mind of the Swiss mercenaries who were serving Holland at the end of the 18th century. Cited by Nicolas Bouvier in *L'Echappée belle, éloge de quelque pèlerins, op. cit.*.

14. Alain Finkielkraut, *L'Humanité perdu*, Seuil. When he wrote "Michelet deposed by Michelin" (i.e., authoritative history replaced by travel guides), on p. 155, one has to hope that the philosopher was exaggerating.

15. Jean-Didier Urbain, *L'Idiot du voyage*, Payot.

16. *L'Humanité perdu, op. cit.*

2.

The Melancholy of the Agité

And what if Agitation is only a disease, the sunny side of a menacing depressive state, haphazardly controlled as we go along? The Agité that I am knows it, feels it, senses it, fears it: the exaltation, the rise toward ecstasy is always quickly followed by the descent into hell. Like any drug experience, the intense feeling of the high from "shooting up" is less significant than the anticipation. It is the desire versus the pleasure. Always pawing the ground, anxious to move. Fury, melancholy. The flamboyant Agité, a decathloner, suddenly has quite livid reflections.

*

* *

The Agité is Exalted

Mountaineers must know this feeling of hyper-oxygenation; a giddiness, a dose of air that is almost like drowning. It is a feeling of a high and at the same time a profound anguish, as if, the lungs filling up with air, the stomach were emptied of its blood and contracted like a fist. An endless loop. The effect is euphoric, elating, rapturous, it is a heartbreaking hit of happiness. You want to be a dancer, you want to dance. Sometimes, to deal with this excess of energy, you have to stand up, stretch your legs, grab the telephone, talk, share. You have to go on the attack in such moments, and find in the whistle of bullets and the promise of their bite one more argument in favor of this exaltation. It is not exactly an absence from the world but a pause, an intermission during which everything is concealed, everything is missing and yet it fills us up. We are filled by the vacuum. We inhale, we get high, we are swallowed up. It's an ecstasy, a mystical chill. You can feel it in cascades, in jolts. Then you are living in a state of minimal apperception, a crystalline touch; you commune in what Henri Michaux tersely summarizes: "Five minutes a day, that is my life." In this state of hyper-awareness, all aflame, it seems unbearable to be alive, to be only mortal; the hyper-acuity becomes a narcosis and the acceleration of thoughts is asphyxiating. Then, in this exceptional moment, the face is suffused with a simple-minded bliss. Then, yes, in our negligible bit of humanity, we feel ready to crush into the same molasses "the pessimism of the intelligence and the optimism of the will" (Gramsci). Before the final collapse.

Exaltation is an avatar of melancholy. That was asserted

centuries ago, with Hippocrates, "humorism" and the theory of the four humors. The complex interplay of the influx and out-flux of black bile and yellow bile has made so much (black) ink flow, it's a pity that we can't use it for blood transfusions. Melancholy, the disease of heroes, has haunted the tragedies since the 4th century BC, and the melancholics show up as what they are: Furies.

"Listen to what an English traveler told me. When the Ashantis decide to wage a war, they start with a solemn ceremony; and an integral part of it requires that the bones of the mother are bathed in human blood. As a prelude to war, the king calls for an attack against his own capital in order to generate some fury."[1]

I love that kind of trick.

Like the society of Iks,[2] whose values seem to be backwards: a mother drops her child and laughs to see it hit its skull on the hard ground. Elsewhere, an old woman falls and rolls in a ditch. She whimpers, unable to get up. Her children go by, laugh, forget her. Mind-boggling cruelty. Agitation of the senses to the point of madness. Theater of the cruel.

The cruelty of families. When Littré was editing his first dictionary, he neglected to note the reference for a quotation that he had used to illustrate a definition. Overcome with remorse, he asked his daughter to find it. One line of Bossuet in 42 volumes! Why this little anecdote? To illustrate their convulsive consultations? Compulsive re-readings? It's a thin line between the exaltation of the conquistador and the despair of the shipwrecked man. A tantalizing threat, like at the Jewish bookseller at Hospitalières-Saint-Gervais, where the works are laid out flat, in piles. To get one from the bottom, you have to move fifty others. Hopefully, you'll read it. A literary imperative. A tyranny.

The Agité is a fury. The enlightened one is dark. His exaltation is an inflexible kind of retrovirus. Every great exalted being is a thwarted depressive. Every great Agité is a candidate for the insane asylum. The writer William Styron's collapse in his hotel room is a warning for those who resemble him, who exhibit and promote his symptoms. Self-confidence, the feeling of success, the gift of observation, multiple interests, panoptical curiosity and a surplus of ideas. . . You're going great guns and then, suddenly, you drop. If you contemplate the sun, you end up blinding yourself.

Speed: a black hole.

I remember the dismay that came over me when I read Styron's description.[3] The further I went in reading about his collapse, the more I felt that my own daily enthusiasm was harboring the worm that was going to ruin my life. The panic that gripped Styron, the fear of having to face a public that was convinced of his glory, spilled over onto me. Yes, for me too, things were definitely going too well.

Here is how the psychoanalyst Juan David Nasio summarizes the cycle of exaltation. The pumped-up, the eclectic, the finger-in-every-pie goes through three successive psychological states: melancholy, anguish, and the instinctive urge to get a grip.

The first phase is depressive. What inspires the active Agité is a state of mourning, the memory of an original loss, of which the wound has remained fresh, like an open sore. These losses may be of any kind, the real loss of a brother, a sister, a relative; bruises from childhood, the feeling of having once been, once too often, too many times, abandoned by one's mother; fear of being deceived (according to the analytical distinction, the fear of abandonment is female, that of deception is male. The woman fears that the father of her children will leave her; the man fears that his children are by a different father). One may also suffer from the loss of a country, a culture, from being up-rooted or exiled, whether it was experienced personally or branded into one's consciousness like a trademark. This family burden, transmitted from generation to generation, becomes a mythic pain. Its resurgence plunges whoever experiences it into anguish.

Anguish is the second stage in the spiraling process that is at the heart of agitation. It leads straight to the next one. To cure this chronic state, this plunge into the abyss, the distressed person has to find a remedy, a substitute for what he has lost and what he is missing. He has to grab onto something: the instinct to mastery.

Because any crisis reactivates the original pain, the original loss, one rushes irrationally toward anything new to mitigate it, to reduce it. One seeks to grasp something that has not yet caused any pain. It is the psychotic version of the poetic neomania of the 18th century. The new relieves us. Alas, this relief is only temporary. The appeasement that it provides is not long in dimming, and it happens more and more quickly. The frequency of substitutions is accelerated and their properties are reduced. We always have to pick up the pace and in the end everything falls to pieces.

The phenomenon is distorted; it produces entropy. Getting used to the sense of loss, fruit of repeated efforts to escape melancholy, contributes to sublimating the world. "I don't enjoy anything anymore" is followed by a refusal to even try. One taste drives out the other or, rather, the tasteless gives way to the odorless. While China may have promoted insipidity to the first dish in any tasting,[4] nothing like that has happened in our latitudes. Rather a dislike has settled in, a lack of appetite.

Le Monde's weather report, November 9. Headline: Agitation. Text: A deep depression.

A twist, inflection of the process, mutation. Soon, you become resigned to living with your suffering. You give up fighting it head-on, you try to tame it. You think that by struggling with the loss more and more often, it will be worn down, it will give in. That by suffering, you will suffer less. One approaches, on a less grandiose scale, the sad motto of the dukes of Mantua: "With neither hope nor fear." All this macabre dance, this highwire display, is intended to mask the final defeat. The process is set in motion in order to avoid seeing the failure that is to come, that which will definitively refuse us the fleeting consolation of a substitute. The much-feared social and physical defeat, the fading of one's charm and charisma, the extinction of the fire against the fine background of the irises, the pallor of the skin, osteoarthritis, thrombosis, age spots, wrinkles. . . No more strength to run, jump, travel, or seduce. . . How can we get used to these smoldering coals that we desperately poke, these glowing embers fire in which our fires are consumed, leading us to pyromania? So-and-so leaves the woman he loves out of fear of losing her; another, madly in love, hops from one bed to another; and a third, afraid of being led on, refuses to love and gives it all up. And the opposite, symmetrical attitude: Don-Juanism as an instinct to master a thousand jolts. Changing partners (if they are tarnished) is equated to a change of décor. Never content.

The dis-eroticization of the world is at work. Everything that is accessible is transferable, everything is reified, it's the reign of the merchandising of love. Under Jean-Jacques Rousseau, commitment gave way to the contract. Living as a couple, making a common life together, used to mean agreeing to gamble on the future (which includes, therefore, accepting the consequences). Today, we break that vow and substitute another as soon as the first one seems not to satisfy us anymore, and our freedom is somewhat vitiated, since it presupposes a will, and we no longer believe in that.

Then this last resort, the ultimate stage where everyone will end up admitting defeat, is in the sack. To counter depression: do it! That's the watchword. The hand that Kant called "external thought" becomes the vehicle by which we apprehend the world. Subjected to a torturous psychic bombardment, the active Agité ends up begging for something else, something new, something more recent. He spurns that which he adored the day before, cutting himself off from the pain by reaching for something passing by. It takes amnesia. To be in "the now." Since Winnicott, we know that the child is weaned when he opens his hand and lets go. The depressive, the melancholic of post-modernity, alienates himself from his own memories, prohibits any analysis, allows himself to be caught by the open tomb of what is presented to him. The famous *hic et nunc*, here and now, has deliberately been made to disappear in favor of the now alone. The development of cyberculture, of the telepresence, only reinforces its domination. It is the great cinema of the cybercity. The hands are clenched, the fists are balled, violence is on the rise. In every agitation, there is disgust.[5] Didn't Sartre want to call his novel *Nausée* "Melancholia"?

Youthism

Grab on, don't let anything go. That's the root of the diseases that are rotting our societies: "youthism," a celebration of the capacity to seize, and commemoration, a statuary travesty of senility. Old, young, not so young, in between: who all imitate the others, in their sneakers. Generalized schizophrenia. They are the same ones who channel and focus their impulses in unbearable ceremonies of memory. The slow passage of the worship of youth, the worship of Agitation, irrational, uncontrolled, into that of the extended life. Then, one celebrates, one moves the ashes. The party is definitely over. Ash Wednesday always follows Mardi Gras. *Carnival*, a word derived from the Tuscan *carnelevare*, means "without meat."[6] After Mardi Gras (literally, "fat Tuesday"), comes emaciation. After the festival, contrition; after the exaltation, the fall and mortification. Youthism and a monument to the dead, a melancholy process followed by the entire society.

Chinoiseries

It also happens that the instinct to mastery can seize up. That the appetite can meet its own downfall. That a tamarind fricassee could defeat the toughest businessman. The decision-makers, the born leaders have their weak point: the Chinese restaurant. When it's time to place their orders, they crack.

Their hyperactive carapace is split to pieces. It is "the resigna-tion phase." This blank stare is the result of a blinding perusal of the infernal and absolutely repetitive list of dishes on the menu. It's always excessive. A mania of our times, and a dis-ease. While their very Asian profusion frankly boils down to some thin slices tossed while still half-alive into some kind of sauce, the wavering client is no longer aware of that. This tem-porary loss of mental equilibrium can occur at "Yang Tsé," "Five Springs," the "Celestial Dragon," in the main dining room, on the terrace, or by the sidewalk. Faced with these flows of pig snouts, cuttlefish fillets, chickens with coconut and stir-fried duck with hearts of palm, the customer implodes. With a guilty voice he stammers, "I don't know what to order," and is plunged into hell. He examines the list, palpates it, and the waiter is al-ready there. You send him away, he comes back in a flash. He takes a moment to uncap the Tsing Tao. He disappears. And here he is, back already! This time the whole table is ready to order: "two #18, one 43, one 34, two 76, no, cross out the 43, I'll take a 76 too. . ." The usual routine, but our decision-maker re-mains undecided. They try to hurry him up. Only making it worse. People in good health, the confident type, know that what you order doesn't matter; what matters is to get it over with as quickly as possible.

Distressed, he is no longer managing anything, not the stir-fried flavors of the food nor the measly potluck platter that they finally give him — some kind of glazed socialist hash. He wants to choose, when he should be escaping. This is what is called reverse agitation, or prostration of the synapses. A petrifying Brownian motion[7] that no dim sum could ever produce. Torture at the street corner is a Chinese specialty.

Always trust the stomach. A traveler returning from Patmos has this to say about his trip. "In Greece, the day you accept a stuffed tomato instead of the stuffed sweet pepper you ordered, the day when you stop going into the kitchen to demand they make the exchange, you are finished. They have you." Then, you have to leave. Greece destroys, devours your dynamic energy. The most Agité of Agités always ends up giving in to sticky moussakas, to the melancholy of the dish *du jour*.

Longitude Lassitude

Long days of lassitude, black spells, fogs. The Agité knows intense fatigues. Deep pits in his exaltation. His chaotic world is riddled with mountains and valleys.

After enthusiastically tackling steep slopes, the fresh wind that reinvigorates and intoxicates, suddenly he hits the quicksand, immobility, a slower tempo, the frustrations of low tide. The Agité, imprisoned in the monotony of his days, doesn't recognize the great descents. He scales cliffs and falls on false plateaus. This gradual slope draws him further in. There is nothing more painful than these moments of implacable depression, monochromic illustrations of Jean Cocteau's maxim, "Life is a horizontal fall." As the flu grips you for eight days without medicine but only for about a week if you take enough prescriptions, these deep dives of depression are drawn out. Three days, as a rule. Someone I know who is from Normandy (and who must be influenced by the damp climate of that region) calls this silting-up "the soft slump." The first day, you feel it coming on. It is perceptible. You were in great shape, full of energy, and here you are caving in. It's not that the sky has turned leaden, with low-hanging clouds, darker, dimmer, but a decline is taking place and the colors are more muted. A grinding sense of conflict sets in. You feel bad, you're anxious, you feel hemmed in, you've lost confidence. The second day, it is obvious, you're in "the slump"! Fatigue, irritability, gloomy predictions, loss of interest, a negative outlook, self-deprecation. The third day is already convalescence, but in intensive care. "The slump" begins to wane, it loosens its grip. You start to relax, to re-emerge, but without energy, warily. . . What if the "slump" comes back, what if it's permanent? So you keep an eye out. You watch yourself for telltale signs, you don't trust yourself. After this trying experience, enthusiasm is gone, punctured, and pollutes everything like the stench of cabbage. It is the odor of the "slump."

This anesthetic pain is a modern version of the Greek term *akedia*, torpor, disinterest, negligence, indifference, tiredness. This weakness of the senses used to be rampant in the monasteries. It haunted the cloisters and the cells. More than one monk was overcome by it, bereft of courage and dissolving into a puddle on his cot, wearied of his solitary life. Breaking his vows, opening breaches in his system, the unfortunate was not satisfied to prostrate himself on the flagstones, unable to move, crushed by the sum of the prayers to be perfected. No, he was agitated. That is the enigma of the *akedia*, the thorn that pricks the sufferer: his torpor is accompanied by an urge to be in action. He has to be busy. The *akedia* is a fatigue that drugs you, dissipates your energies while prodding you to action, a trance, a kind of "Baudelairian spleen." "*Akedia*, for the monk, is a death that comes at him from all sides."[7] But aren't we, too, victims of this strange malady? The frustrated, solitary Agité, surrounded by multiple multifaceted connections, walled in by the humming of computer screens, the wail of the modem, email, chat groups, and the infinite Web, slip-sliding away on the heavy and cunning flip-side of the disenchantment of the world?

Footnotes

1. G.W.F. Hegel, *Leçons sur la philosophie de l'histoire*, Vrin, p. 91.

2. Hake Turnbull, *Iks. Survivre par la cruauté. Nord Ouganda*, the Terre humain collection , Plon.

3. William Styron, *Face aux Tenebres*, Gallimard.

4. François Jullien, *Eloge de la fadeur*, Editions Philippe Picquier.

5. And as Bernanos so nicely puts it, "As long as there is fear, anything is possible, but when disgust occurs, it's finished."

6. Jean Clair, *Le Nez de Giacometti*, Gallimard, p. 67.

7. Brownian motion: the random movement of microscopic particles suspended in liquids or gases when they are hit by molecules of the surrounding fluid.

8. Saint Jean Climaque. Cited by Jean-Louis Christian in his chapter on Akedia in *De la fatigue*, Minuit.

Part Two

THE WORLD AT THE MERCY OF THE AGITÉ

1.

The Agité as a Seismograph

Enough whining. Melancholy doesn't explain everything. The acceleration of the world is a fact and the Agité is agitated mostlyy because he's trying to keep up, to deal with the sudden convulsions of the whole planet, to keep pace with the seismograph.

As if he had been tossed into the test-tube of an era of explosive reactions, he precipitates. That's his alchemy.

Neurasthenics, strap in! Because melancholy was included in the quarrels of our ancestors, it has been graced with the solemnity of antiquity. We would hold it to be sovereign, immutable, everlasting. That's wrong. It, too, is about to be swept away. Rocked, kicked into the end zone. Manhandled by speed. If the Agité is agitated, it's because he is jousting on all sides. The planetary coconut tree is being shaken by conflicts and combats. The question, "Why is the world changing?" has been replaced by "How can we live in a world that has become unrecognizable?" A panoptical patchwork, a wide-angle lens. See everything and say everything. The Agité understands it all too well. Instinct for mastery or no, he likes to think he's up to date on everything new. If it's more powerful than he is, he's interested. It is wonderful.

An ultravert but tight as a fist, the Agité cannot resist the whirling of the dervish that spins his world. He is subject to electrolytic conversion. If he attains wisdom, it is through vibration. Rhythm speaks to him more than melody, the alternation of sounds and silences more than the celestial yawns expectorated by the yogis and all their bodily manifestations. He prefers the jazzman over the zazen,* the steeplechase over the parade.

To tell the truth, to express his expansiveness, his sudden spurts and impulses, a CD-ROM or even a simple web page would be more useful than all the sentences we could put together. Because, in fact, the additions aren't the point, rather it is the accumulation, the superposition. Another liability of writing, trapped as it is in its pages and its binding. If you juxtapose the enigma of the main entrance to a condo building (the gateway to so many unsuspected dramas) and the much-

* A form of Buddhist meditation

proclaimed gateway to cyberspace, if you superimpose tattered fringes of emerging cities (territories that are expanding without any center or plan) and the infinitude of the universe, there is a whole palpitating world that remains to be grasped and explained. The rubric "city," with a simple click, the blink of an eye, has been expanded with the ultramodern concept of the "Brazilianization of the world." The Agité dances the samba.

Under the impetus of Faith Popcorn (self-proclaimed priestess of trends, mother of the popular term *cocooning*), *bunkering* came in and then it, too, vanished. "I stay home," the trend for a few years, was followed by "I stay home and *I don't see anybody anymore*;" that was a dose of hemlock, a suicidal potion. The individual approach came to a dead end. No one is sufficiently morbid to be buried alive just to go along with fashion. Then, leaving Rio de Janeiro, the evolving concept of bunkering was renamed with the exotic and misleading term of "Brazilianization," and extended its archipelago. Today, it is corroding the surface of the globe. The family unit is giving way to compact communities of individual units all cut off from each other, behind their gate houses. Their fortunes threatened by crime, all these girdled worlds surrounded with trash, encircled by *favelas* (Brazilian shantytowns), opt for ironwork and the crenellations of enclosure; they are the descendants of medieval walled cities, now with a network of cameras and electronic sensors to devour the night.

"Bunkerization," "Brazilianization," the neologisms that

pop like corn kernels thrown in the pan, sink into an abyss and give birth to one another. For this Brazilianization of the world is echoed by the "slumification" of the world, the carcinogenic deployment of tentacular universes of infinitely extended conurbations, on-off ramps, parking lots, hotels, airports, shopping centers, houses, ghettos, repetitive entities butting up against not just the wealthy neighborhoods anymore but whole cities, a patchwork of private jurisdictions. The wave breaks, from California to Nevada, Arizona to Caracas, Bogota to Buenos Aires and Mexico City. So many little islands of prosperity at sea amongst the decrepit. During the 1996 Architecture Bienniale in Venice, while Japan was exhibiting the open wounds in Kobe, exhibiting in its pavilion giant photographs of all the gaping seismic holes, the United States, in a provocative and calculated nonchalance, displayed the achievements of Disney's leaders of "Corporate-Design." And one suddenly guessed, in this universe of giant delights, that the world to come would be like this: two sharply distinct theme parks. The first one charges a fee and is super-protected, offering sensations and thrills to the crowd of the secure in measured doses according to their wishes, in closed and controlled universes; and the second, the real park of terror, free from the restraints of law, is accessible only to those who have guns or an overdose of adrenalin. In these ungovernable suburbs, with no admission fee but left to the anarchy of the gangs, people will be killing each other purely gratuitously. Murder, a gratuitous act that seemed surrealist only yesterday, used to be committed close-range on the sidewalk; from now on, it will be large-scale, between two highway access ramps, at a chance meeting. And we already have the name for it: *drive-by shooting.* Assassination at full speed, bullets and tires screaming. Shhhh...., they're coming back.

Pop Art? No, Popcorn

Clickety-click. With every new click, a crossroads. The spirit of the age, running at lightning speed, cannot contain its incendiary connections. With a great burst of flames, they overwhelm all of our proofs, carbonize our certainty. Thus the ridiculous moniker "Faith Popcorn" is well-suited to the outrageous propositions that this guru hammers home like so many revelations in her last prophetic work, aptly entitled *Clicking.*[1] Her sayings: "The 21st century will be feminine," "genealogy will rule the world," and others, are greeted like oracular pronouncements. But by a twist of fate, an inopportune slip of the mouse, while clicking directly on the popcorn you can suddenly find yourself in a world of fractals. The cannonade of kernels let loose in the microwave comes back to us like an echo of the air-conditioned offices of Walt Disney Corp. in Los Angeles. There, groups of creatives in shirtsleeves are slaving away on the globalization of the next rodent intrigue. Between pizzas and sushi brought by a continuous parade of deliverymen, and pyramids of Diet Coke cans, they suck in mountains of popcorn. Behind them, somewhere behind a partition, an explosive device is detonating all day long to produce this harvest. From pop to pop, the sense of value disappears, the sense of reality is lost. Our judgment is blunted. We crumble under the onslaught. The panes crack, break, fracture. From "bunkerization" to popcorn, we are picking up speed. We are diving into the gleaming universe of Mandelbraut's fractals, for the kernel contains the popcorn as surely as the frog contains the tadpole, and the layout of a supermarket, the display cases that start and finish every row. The infinitesimal is mimicking us. It, too, vibrates with constant trepidation, its molecules dance, its ions are irritated, its trifling structures are shaken by an irrepressible breath of life. By successive changes of scale, the most complex combinations result one from the other. A Brownian movement shakes it all up. It is a fashionable cacophony of micro-spaces that are divided, subdivided, and automated. This disturbed schizogenesis (splitting of intercellular spaces) admirably illustrates Joseph Brodsky's reflection, "If there is an infinite line in space, it is not due to the possibility of expansion but rather of contraction."[2] The triumph of miniaturization.

These Territories that are Popping Up, What Shape are They?

In classical thought, the world was considered an ensemble of simple geometries, a square, a sphere, a circle... Thus, to live in harmony, architects should build habitats along the same lines. During the inauguration of I. M. Pei's pyramid at the Louvre, François Mitterrand declared, "All great architecture is sim-

ple." He thus spoke for the most extreme, and even blunt, classi-
cism. Promoter of a circle at the Opera of the Bastille, of a
square at the Grande Arche and a pyramid where we just men-
tioned, he was also the architect of a simplistic purification.[3]

With fractals, it is another story. Once we have acknowledge that the world, far from being a stable universe of fixed
forms, is a conglomeration of feverish ions with considerable
potentialities, we can start to guess at the vastness of all that is
staring us in the face. Now, we'll have to build dynamic, complex buildings, agitated by innumerable hiccups and firing self-
generated burps at each other. An audacious program is under-
way to experiment with static limits. The architects of the
Coop Himelblau Group in Vienna (Austria) are playing with
breaking up the main spaces, while in Japan, Peter Eisenman is
designing "post-seismic" buildings with the floors tilted on an
angle, in anticipation of the earthquake, and then there is Frank
Gehry, with his Guggenheim museum in Bilbao.

Charles Jencks, to whom we owe the concept of postmod-
ernism — a paternity that Jean-François Lyotard disputes —
tried to give Agitation concrete form in the U.K.. An undeniably
brave experiment. At his manor in Scotland, on a relentlessly
green moor, he built a living room and a gazebo in strict accordance with Mandelbraut's theories. In the living room, the
doors and blinds are set at angles whose logic escapes us. Only
the effect counts. A kitchen unit is decorated with a bizarre,
ramified and complex formula describing the reproduction of

rabbits, an obscure algebraic note but of considerable topicality in a province where these small beasts thrive and proliferate. Elsewhere, the contorted silhouettes of the coffee tables take their inspiration from the twisting motion of a wave that, like a criminal, retraces its path, in the wake of the chisel that stems the wave and makes it break. Got that?

Charles Jencks summarizes and encapsulates this admirable effort in a concise aphorism that is both irritating and captivating. "Today, the whole question is to figure out what form to give to the precise moment when the grain of corn becomes popcorn." Remarkable. A perpetual double bang.

Back to square one, and the corners are sharp.

The Universe Has a Grain

To describe a grain of corn is within the capabilities of any student trained in the mysteries of classical thought. The corn kernel adheres to simple geometrics. It starts out looking like a cube, but has an elongated brownish shell. But how would you describe popcorn? Exploded, toric, epsilonian? The apparent simplicity of the question, and its apparently minimal risk suck you in. It is a serious question, bursting with health, explosive. The seed of Agitation.

At one time the corkscrew, the quintessential perfect technical object, also required the support of a drawing, in order to become more widely adopted. There's nothing like a good diagram to explain to the beginner how to operate this formidably

French utensil. Where endless descriptions and instructions only damp the spirit and discourage the actor, already ripened by the tannins and the perfume, a good drawing says everything. Only, look! Since complexity governs the world, popcorn refuses to be diagrammed. It is a mutant that, to reveal itself, requires the support of both an image and a sound. It is an object of poisonous study. The casual witness, in his naiveté, thinks that watching is all it takes to understand. However, the unplanned contemplation of a falling apple never helped anyone (except you-know-who) to deduce the contorted mechanisms of terrestrial attraction. The falling apple requires an explanation. Our popcorn is the corkscrew of the virtual era. Its emphatic backfire is like the echo of the vague snapping sound of Bordeaux grapes being sacrificed. The explanation goes nowhere, the drawing looks wrong. This time, only the image, strained though it may be, comes anywhere close to depicting the troublesome reality. But the movement is missing. And the explosion. In the murky shadows of the centuries, this artistic vagueness is a kind of admission. The Agité who fidgets and crackles is the kernel, just waiting to be ignited so he can blast off.

We don't give popcorn enough consideration.

Simultaneism

The oscillations of modernity are increasing in amplitude. Every undulation of the trampoline tosses us a little higher and gives us a glimpse of previously unsuspected territories, new worlds. Every rebound erodes our old landmarks. In a universe where sailing from one site to another no longer requires orienting yourself to the two poles, terrestrial attraction becomes a matter of hypothesis. The foundations no longer exist. Any child equipped with a "playstation 64" (or similar) knows that. The virtual world allows you to change your perspective. Above, below, head-on, in the cockpit, we are having a great garage sale giving away the foundations. Feet to the wall, or beyond the walls. Thus, to handle the flashes of our thoughts, we have to rely on our spiritual connections, erect a system that can stand up to the super-abundance of supply. If not, seized with giddiness like an icon collector thrown into hidden cache of unsuspected treasures, we will end up suffocating in the dust as we stir things up, blinded by the grit kicked up by the hallucinatory beat of microscopic electronic impulses. You can also die from being crushed by your virtual library.

Several Stories, but I'll Tell only One of Them

When, going from Angoulême to Chateauroux, one counted in terms of days on the mail coach, Roman linearity was justification enough. Now our lives, beset with a multiplicity of demands, are not satisfied with anything less than a senator's life style. The American writers understood that sooner than others, for it is in their nature, in their Americanity, to be on the move. In the United States, the export of values and patriotism is tautological. The Jim Harrisons, the Richard Fords, the Paul Austers are representatives of a current in writing that is almost a flood. Quentin Tarantino, Robert Altman, Woody Allen, manipulators of images, from editing to final cut, have popularized the genre. To tell one story, it helps to tell several. The narratives support each other, illustrate each other, play like the facets of a single crystal, and display one single humanity in all their reflections. These flashes of culture are our mirror. Already, in the 1930's, Eisenstein filmed in short sequences because the war prevented his working for long periods. War, nuclear deterrence. By the 1950's, the end of the world became an end in itself. Cinema started to gasp. Humanity was not so much living as surviving. Today, we live innuclear fission, the great nuclear *frisson*.

Ryszard Kapuscinski, the Polish reporter who emigrated to Berlin, wrote two masterpieces that bear the traces of this. In *The Shah* and *The Négus,* he captured in a myriad of brushstrokes the Pompeian portrait of a two-fold collapse. This is no more a matter of literary pointillism. While Kapuscinski researched every aspect of this terrain for over ten years, to boil it down in the end to just one hundred pages, he did not compose one simple painting but a series of frescos, each element of which is the "booster rocket" of the others. An agitation of particles. Then perhaps we should talk about simultaneism, the most apt term for describing this new way in which we apprehend the world and those who propel themselves through it, fidget in it and survive in it, starting with ourselves.

The linearity of all life escapes us. The falls and rebounds, anticipations and hopes make each existence a blazing inferno. Each one a drama. We all live at several different rhythms, simultaneously. First is the long, romantic sense of time. The time of founding families, of filiations, heritages. Then, over a time shorter, crammed with activities planned, envisaged, and carried out; medium-term prospects, various commitments that are essential but can be put off; and, finally, in a short, desperately accelerated timeframe where urgency determines what is important, where the stress of decision-making is blinding. All these levels are interwoven and overlapping. Paul Virilio used the excellent image of simultaneous "under-exposure, exposure, over-exposure." Any exchange contains all three. The ease of casual conversation, the tension of insinuations, repressions, objectives, rancor. A man and a woman. Their attraction and their private life, their family relations and offspring, and the temptation to chuck it all and leave, to set out again from square one. The simultaneity of monumental constraints, one hidden inside another, the mortar that reinforces the exchanges and interrelations of beings, bringing them together and dispersing them. The vapor of existence.

We had become Cubist constructions, all here simultaneously, in an insect's thousand-faceted view. The theory of the points of view, used in literature, is no longer relevant. The interleaved and opposing narratives, the brilliance deployed by Lawrence Durrell in his *Alexandria Quartet*, do not belong to our times. The points of view are in each one of us, superimposed, and always contradictory. Hell is other people; our other selves, cenotaphs of our feelings that are embalmed, then re-appear, like the floodplains of the Nile. Catastrophic but fertile.

Even better than the instantaneous (which dissolves), the punch of the simultaneous. It is a caffeine boost, a drop kick of energy. It is a cup that we stir and swallow in order to drown in it. A shared bowl of air, a collective hyperventilation.

You see a guy running down the sidewalk, in a sweat, exhausted. He complains, but keeps going. Another person, who is considering calling it quits, giving it up, hesitates. Somebody else pops up unexpectedly and shakes open his newspaper, meanwhile cranking up the radio. No time to lose. Here is some froth, collected at the bar. They all have something in common: they live as though they were inside a washing machine. No longer layering one on top of another like a pile of Turkish carpets, but interleaved, braided together, woven, tugged and pulled like indestructible Gore-Tex.

Is this a coincidence that the clothes-wringer is used more and more often as part of the window-dressing at the couturier Paco Rabanne, on rue du Cherche-Midi in Paris, and above the bar designed by Tom Dixon in Leeds, not to mention in Shibuya's department store windows in Tokyo?

It's 5:00 PM, Do You Still Know Who You Are?

Just as a Cubism of vision and a deconstructivism of thought developed, now we are seeing the advent of a simultaneism of active life. But from this sudden wealth a nagging discouragement wells up. Nothing is harder than defining oneself. Who are we? Who am I? Now, yesterday, tomorrow? The delicate question requires an answer because of today's requirement that we make a generalized confession, that we reveal ourselves and grovel before society as a whole. Everywhere is the injunction of the transparency. This complete exposure is actually a paradox, a trick; it imprisons. You would have to not hide anything at all, in order for appearances to be true. And then there are those exasperating expressions, "a real relationship," "a genuine talent," "a real desire." Then you start to stammer. You backtrack, start to contradict yourself, add something, delete something, honing and refining the image, polishing and interpolating. Every assertion is counterbalanced by another, weakening it, putting it in perspective, reducing its impact. "I love baklava," says one person, "but I prefer Turkish delight; in fact, on reflection Turkish delight is definitely superior to baklava." Under the pretext of telling all, of frankness, it is indecision that comes out. We adopt a thousand positions in order to avoid choosing any single one, knowing that the only way to overcome desire is to deceive ourselves that we are free. Especially to give ourselves the impression that we are making a free choice (since that is what it means to rule). Anorexic or bulimic? Anorexic *and* bulimic! At the same time. Here are some oxymorons: "I am a night watchman, and a writer," "a mechanic and a video producer," "faithful, and in love with all women," "I am a woman, and a mother," "Pisces and Libra." The bartender whose attention is so hard get when you want to order a drink has many excuses. Sure, he is a waiter, but at the same time he is a serious body-builder, a peerless competitor in motorcycle shows, a painter who exhibits his work outside the city, and an expert in philately. How's that for simultaneity!

Inherent in this taxidermic self-revelation, in this subservience that makes the lie detector useful only in a game show, we risk being cooped up in the dark room of a blind modernity. Always having to find something to say, always having to expose ourselves. And worse yet, feeling our own identity eluding us, losing sight of who we are.

It's a small step from exposure to over-exposure, from appearance to disappearance. Every photographer knows it: if you reveal too much, you end up destroying any image. And this is even truer of stereotypes.

Buildings in Motion

Superposition is a fact of life. We have to deal with it. I will be accused of weakness, of giving in. Don't speak too soon. No, the path is open for all sorts of experimentation with other ways to relate to the world. A little talent, a little audacity. Push, try, seek. The architect Francis Soler's awful Library, decorated with a modern mishmash that looks like wilted flowers, for example. He designed a building whose picture windows have images silk-screened onto them. From the inside, if you look out toward the horizon, you see a Parisian sky studded with cherubs and haloed Virgins. From the outside, when by chance the sun strikes the façade, you get an explosion of frescos, a *quattrocento* bazaar, neo-kitsch and striking; a kind of comic strip from Martin's Home Decoration Centers. Soler did not substitute an outspoken tattooing for the insignificance of the translucent glass façades, he implemented his theory of focal distances as the guiding principle *Ubiquité oblige*, simultaneism at all times; he wanted to build the multiplicity of points of view, and without giving fuel to today's tendency to argue that a varied discourse is only a mask for inconsistency, and chaos a pretext for incoherence.

The Advent of Zoom-Man

The time of head-on assaults is over; contemplative unity is finished. Our brain, like a good Japanese zoom lens, is moving in and out. For the man of art, it's no longer a question of designing charming buildings that please the eye of the idle by-stander, but of plastering the city with sensitive plates, integrating remote and up-close images, real and simulated. Francis Soler, in his own way, is a crusader for Agitation. His combat is redemptive. He wants to get the TV-viewer out of his armchair and, with this intention, he is filling the city with surprising buildings like so many works of art that have to be seen in person. The enemy is the screen (whether computer or television) that displays a world not of condemnable hoaxes but of synthetic paradises that are more attractive, more amusing than the morose reality of the sordid and uninspiring streets. If Soler is working on it, it is not to soften it but to smite it. Multiplying the points of view, multiplying the vanishing points, he uses a *camera obscura* device on wheels. Soler's work thus derives specifically from his field of endeavor. It is a high-stakes game, seeking to infuse movement into architecture, a discipline which is essentially static, which is above all an art of foundation and mass. It is a wandering trajectory, a spring-loaded dolly.

The Method

Apply the theory of focal distances all the time. Change lenses, move. Vertigo. In front of me, I see on the wall the "U" and the "S" that summarize an entire nation; and then suddenly, zoom back and dissolve: US, "us." This country has powerful initials that signify the entire community.

Echoes

Agitation of the senses. Under the title, "S M L XL," the Dutch architect and guru Rem Koolhaas describes in his book the multi-tentacled explosion of global cities. He takes a perverse joy in Chinese "mushroom cities," in violence as a development tool — a creed that is hinted at in the "S M" (for sadomasochism) in the title and is further registered in the text. The medievalist Michel Pastoureau points out to me that in China, to indicate "great," or "many," one said "10,000" (the Emperor had 10,000 concubines, the Wall of China is 10,000 leagues long); in imperial Rome, the number "40" was used the same way. However, 40 written in Roman numerals is XL. Under tee-shirt imperialism, that made Rome, quite simply, the extra-large empire.

Cyber

So yes, to avoid indigestion, adjust your zoom lens and focus on the world that is slipping away and disappearing. And in the meantime, in mid-swing in this piston motion that flips us from one point of view to another, suddenly recognize the interloper that makes it all possible. Everything seems normal behind the paneling. And yet, behind the double windows of our old neogothic building, in the walls, beneath the floors, in the air, data is constantly flowing; waves of information, electrical currents, electronic jokes are crossing and intersecting. It is an infinity of telescoping, of telereporting. Satellites, radio-TV. . . Without even realizing it, we are constantly immersed in an omnipresent virtuality.

Not long ago, we kept our savings nodding in sleeping bank accounts. In those days, a bank was something solid, a marble construction, a massive block festooned with firm-breasted caryatids and the muscled chests and trunks of telamones. Back then, we had confidence in bankers. Then the branch office was reduced to a drive-in teller's window, to a telephone number, and finally to a simple card embedded with a computer chip. And this computer became portable. Relaxed, melting into the beach, between sun lotion and inflatable raft, we can summon it to the screen with a simple "click." Carefree, we have plunged, in our bathing suits, into the first level of cyberspace.

Since then, that architecture on the verge of extinction has re-emerged in computer buffs' jokes. Synthesized images, special effects, computer-generated neo-pop stars. . . the plot thickens, and it's a cyber-plot. Soon, you can be sure, cyber-architecture will re-appear on the ground. We will live in liquid expanses, fluids and flows. Space will take human form. In man's image, it will have to disappear, fade away. And we won't trust it any more than we trust our nearest neighbor.

What is constant, in reality, tomorrow in the virtual universe will be replaced by variables. Finally. For, to tell the truth, nothing in our hard physical reality is constant. Durability, like hardness, are figments of the mind. Ambition is a hair shirt. To remind us of our "vanity."

The virtual is closer to reality than reality itself.

Blips

The reason the modernization program did so much harm to the French national rail system is because its promoters tried to superimpose a digital system on top of an analog system (sales counters, tickets, trains, rails, stations. . .) like the one that was implemented long since in the airports. One more cataclysm of acceleration. The difference between the train and the plane is exactly the same as the gap that is growing ever wider between the analog and digital worlds. In the train, the user gets up and goes to look for something to eat and drink. The bar car is located as far as possible away from the travelers. On the airplane, you have to wait in your seat until you are served. A nomad in the train, you become chair-bound on the plane. Eurostar breaks the rule. With the eating-at-your-seat system, the first class passenger now has to wait until someone brings him his meal. Thus, he has lost the use of his legs. Actually, he has lost far more for, insidiously, he has also been deprived of the landscape, poetry, Cendrars and even Siberia and the conquest of the West.

A train trip used to be an adventure, a great pleasure. You could enjoy the landscape. The new rapid trains are taking that away. Now, everything goes by too quickly and at this speed, the train is going through a uniform continuum. In short, you end up walking around because there is nothing to see any more. Now, the interval between one station and another is like the transit between two airports. The windows of the TGV look out on the same nothingness as a ship's porthole. In other words, as they say in the digital universe, between blips (stations, airports, or the seconds whizzing by on the dial), there is nothing left anymore. "Digital" is the disappearance of intervals.

Giving rise to the question, If travel is not enough any

more, does being agitated consist in finding intermediate spaces?

Popscape

Without even realizing it, the crowd is already passing briskly from analog to digital with the same thrill that yesterday led them from the factory to the beach.

In spite of how we curse and disparage the new gathering places, the public seems to be voting in their favor. In the supermarkets and malls, they seem to be finding what the Sixties generation came to look for in the airports: communion with the cosmos, a palpable perception of the great cosmic flow. Slogans, signs, lights, music, continuous surges of goods in continuous motion, the ebb and flow of the crowds, flags, wind, noise, performers, parking lots, the feeling of being collectively caught up in spaces under tension, of taking part in the great movements of the world — everything that the universe of the electromagnetic glorifies. In this popscape, this popular electronic landscape, something is always happening. Monolithic architecture has had its day; now, the doorways are many, and the public is exhaled into the maze of grocery shelves, the 3-D counterparts of the computer screen. The supermarket windows are already built in Hypertext. The customer, with just one click, enters a data warehouse. Before him, all around him, the goods, detergents, fruit and vegetables, cosmetics and appliances, appear without intermediary. Everything is within hand's reach, in real time, live. The supermarket provides direct access to the digital limbo, to the yes/no of programming, with bar codes over every item. The Sunday Mass isn't so impressive, anymore, when you compare it to this undeniable condensing communion of modernity. The customer, with his beatific smile, pushing his cart down the aisle, could show a thing or two to any professional futurologist. Advanced technologies? He practices them already, at least once a week and with his whole family.

All the same, isn't this passion for vaulted hangars in primary colors against a background of parking lots the lowest level of the love of junk? An effect of the "trash culture," the nirvana of recycling, persistent approval of all that modernity mass produces, without worrying about durability? TV esthetics, the vulgar, the victory of the crude, the coarse, the hard, the low-end? Maybe. Fascination with the cheap is a fact of life at the turn of the century. Walter Benjamin summarized this position when he pessimistically prophesied: "Humanity has become a stranger to itself, by succeeding to experience its own destruction as an aesthetic pleasure of the first order."

Societal cynicism of the nuclear age, a way of neglecting our capacity to self-destruct, or more surely the birth of a new world?

Seeing things without being too judgmental. The Agité takes that gamble. He takes risks. In France, that isn't looked upon too favorably.

Mind-Boggling

Now, even space is subjected to deregulation. Border disputes are overflowing just like our garbage dumps. Moreover, and as is the case in any sensitive neighborhood, refuse causes conflict. It smells bad. Rather than down the stairwells and out the windows, conflicting scientific experts are throwing trash at each other. The days are gone when you could measure the population's well-being by the volume of their country's waste. Gradually, as more satellites are launched and more materials are jettisoned, the cosmos, the only one we have, is filling up with detritus. On their courses through the galactic expanse, spacecrafts now have to zigzag between wrecks. To reduce the risks of an accident, shuttles fly backwards and upside down — which in itself amounts to a state of weightlessness — in order to interpose the maximum mass between the crew (and the capsule's vital systems) and any object that might smash into them. It's a bad environment. At the speed of 15,000 mph, a 0.004-inch fleck of metal will pierce a spacesuit; at the size of 0.02 inches, it will notch a window on the shuttle. In fact, NASA has already had to replace 63 port-holes on its space vehicles. At a per unit cost of $40,000, that makes for an expensive load of trash.

The world is getting smaller, but denser. Perceptibly so.

Full Steam Ahead

A few years ago, the expression "vaporware" came into vogue; in a flash, it was propagated by the tribe of computer programmers and thousands of neurotic subscribers to the worldwide "network" made a fortune on it. Between software and hardware, a vague and elusive notion cropped up, imperceptible but omnipresent, the hint of software yet to come, conceived but not yet produced, just evoked, dreamt up, promised. The enlightened ones of the Web, in their obscure techno-dialect, had hit the jackpot. For *vaporware* sums up in one word everything that is taking over a society that is governed by electronic pulses, global connections and exchanges that are invisible to the naked eye: dirty money, the lobbies, the Mafias, the cults, viral proliferations, and the entire AIDS epidemic. By proclaiming the supremacy of a controlled vaporware, these internauts thought they are working for democracy. They thought they were lighting the backfire that would block the wildfire, would disperse the vague mass of occult powers that were beyond the citizens' control.

Threats to democracy are increasing, and the Web should counterbalance that. Nice thought, but off-base. The schizophrenics get fired up and chase after bits lost in the new Atlantis of computing; the paranoiacs choke. It all makes great grist for the conspiracy theorists. Any isolated act becomes the missing link in a great attack by the sinister forces that stalk throughout the universe, omniscient. And everyone is up in arms with denunciations. The Web, while waiting for the great skybridge bristling with satellites, is a magnet for alarmist testimonies. Conference centers are boiling with them: assassination plots against the pope; poisoning of the food supply; the diabolical design of a certain model of sports car or juice-maker, or a company's head office and logo, are identified and denounced as being extraterrestrials in disguise. Agitation verges on panic. *Vaporware* as a fog is becoming solidified.

Vaporware is the modern version of the ultra-kitsch Tupperware ceremony. In the 1950's and 1960's, the respectable ladies of good American society met at these events and citizen networks were formed. Besides the objective of selling boxes and selling the illusion of conservation and economy — everyone knows that Tupperware is good for preserving today what you're going to throw out anyway four days later — these housewives were induced to reveal their intimate problems, hitherto hidden in the bosom of the families. With its hermetic plastic containers and lids, Tupperware opened the way to feminism. Apparently, conservation leads to revolution.

Tupperware also heralded another revolution, the disappearance of forms. By celebrating the advent of plastic, these translucent boxes consecrated the supremacy of the polished over the crude. Before the invention of plastic injection molds, everything that was stamped man-made was "polished," smoothed by hand. Nature only provided things in the rough. In the 1950's, that perception was reversed. The mold, consecrating the victory of mass production, did away with the concept of "polish." Consequently, and in reaction against these smooth, machined, assembly-line products, the West became infatuated with crude art. Everything that was raw, rough, lumpy, angular found an audience. Collections of African art, crystals and minerals, and burled wood were adopted as interior decoration by the jet-set aesthetes. Today, a crude guy is certainly a nuisance but at least he "has personality"; and a smooth character seems sleazy.

Vaporware has put an end to this competition. It closes a chapter in the war between the crude and the polished. Fading into the azure, it transcends all material conflicts and appears only to be some kind of ethereal deification. Rebelling against all forms of organization, the crowd threw itself body and soul into the bizarre, the shocking, the incredible. No one demonstrated this better than the punks, with their slam dancing, scuffling and half-falling on the dance floor. This time, instead of hurling the usual pejoratives, no one makes any sign at all. It is other-worldliness. Jean-Charles de Castelbajac's success as a couturier is partially explained by the naivety of his line, his athletic-looking models, his screaming hues, his use of solid colors — evocations of a reassuring heraldry. Clean, tidy and noxious. Vapor, and irreproachable.

Cuckoo, It's Me Again

In his own way, the Agité is a nebula. He is everywhere, hidden behind the mask of his pseudonyms, broadcasting on multiple wavelengths, vibrating, a whirling dervish in schizogenesis, an "institution unto himself." People try to peg him with so many labels, so many crude neologisms (since our traditional vocabulary balks at trying to pigeonhole him). First the word was "Multi," used initially in Japan; then "Omni," a little more dissipated, dispersed, omnipresent, ubiquitous, international. At this rate, the expanding Agité is likely to explode. Cloning on every level the floors; a personality milkshake, crime of the ego in an intimate vapor. To be a battalion in and of oneself, all alone, a nebula, a "webula" of networks. Will we soon see troops of Agités, multitudes always ready to pay their various characters to sniff the world with all their sensitive sensors? And will we see, tomorrow, the contemplative revanchists generated in laboratories, the physical incarnations of Buddhas, one more full of horse shit than another, a mystical symphony of annoying people set loose in corporate corridors, truckloads of persecutors brought in to make life difficult for the disgraced Agités? Fist loads of knuckleheads. Nightmare of nightmares.

Cursed Vapor

The name of the USSR was one of the most distressing instances of the de-territorialization discussed by Deleuze and Guattari.[4] For the first time, a country was baptized with an acronym, a name that did not refer to any precise geographical space. The Union of the Soviet Socialist Republics could unleash its steamroller across the whole earth. By creating a country that was nowhere in specific, in the hope that it could be everywhere, eventually — a country without an anchor — it

was already *vaporware*. A country as tightly closed as Tupperware but spreading like a cursed vapor, that same vapor that
already in 1913, in the adventures of abominable Fu Manchu,
slipped under a door to assassinate a hapless London scientist.[5]
A vapor that already heralded the gas attacks 1914 and the universe of Nazi concentration caps and the gulags. Black order,
green vapor, yellow peril, red terror.

Tidal Waves

Those who venerated the Agitation squared, the madness
cubed, the energy explosion of Hong Kong (whose retrocession
at midnight June 30, 1997 was the "lead" story on all the
"leading" news programs throughout the world), have not made
the pilgrimage to the thalweg frontier of the New Territories. A
venerable river used to flow there, cleaving the Chinese soil in
two, isolated the colonial concession of the south from the imperial vastness to the north. A free zone, a *non aedificandi* zone,
virgin land girdled with barbed wire and overlooked, on the
Hong Kong side, by a gazebo. From this perch British potentates and residents nostalgic for the motherland came to survey
the other, formidable, side.

An old postcard from the Sixties shows that, during the
Cold War, there was nothing on either side of this channel but
bucolic and militarized greenery. One of those lethal no man's
lands where the least step out of line will ignite the windy silence with the terminal staccato of machine-guns.

About thirty years later, in that much bally-hoo'd spring, I went up to the summit. What a shock! Imagine a rival peak, a wall, a barrier of buildings, a menacing horde of construction sites, earthmovers brandished in the face of the British concession like the guns of a tank, the jaws of excavating machines baring their teeth. There, extending to the horizon, surging up like a bubbling swell, was the tidal wave of Shenzhen, an epileptic and proliferating city, the first wave of a frontal attack.

For in the Hong Kong underbrush, along the narrow paths, in obscure recesses between trees, on the close-cropped grass of the few remaining meadows, the Fifth Column was lying low. Working under cover, under the camouflage of tarps, heaps of building materials, bricks and cinder blocks, bulldozers, cranes, and dump trucks repainted overnight. . . Equipment stored in anticipation of D-day. Everything was set for the great event, for the great take-off, the Great Leap Forward. Let the river cease for one moment being the legal *caesura* and in one shot, the autophage madness of this territory would cross the line and change sides. Shenzhen, already connected to Guangzhou (Canton), would be linked to Kowloon and then to Hong Kong, by a stroke of the pen, by a load of cement. Dust as destiny, a downhill trend worldwide. Between the Schengen Accords* and the thundering dis-accords of Shenzhen, there is no "photo op"; there isn't room for everyone in the final shot. In place of the Chinese of yesteryear, in their tuxedos and silken robes, the

---

* granting free circulation of people and goods throughout signatory countries in Europe

territory given over to the vibrations of caterpillars will soon welcome nothing but the sweat of coolies and the billionaire deal-makers specializing in the famous local product: concubines, as special as the region itself, an administrative entity where progress itself is ejaculating.

A little further, a little later, at the same locale, in the New Territories. A private investor has built on a forest of concrete pillars a hundred kilometers of highway, complete with access ramps. For the time being, the surrounding territory is naked. There's nothing. Not a city, not an industry, not even a "zoning plan." Just this useless snake. Come back in five years. The ground will have been subdivided, sold, developed, occupied, parcelled out to factories with their polluting smokestacks, to fast-food outlets and drug stores, to thousands of residential skyscrapers. The investment will have been repaid a hundred times over; in spite of a hundred crises.

In Pudong, Shanghai's flashy new district, 80% of the highrise office buildings that were put up one after the other in the enthusiasm of the capitalist revolution seem to be vacant. In the reflux of Asian stagnation, they represent a *vaporware* in which bankruptcies suddenly ruin all certainty.

Vaporware everywhere. General agitation. A palpable acceleration. If technologies are smoke screens, there's no smoke without fire. In the putrid recesses of the planet, in the folds of the Geological Survey maps, miniaturization and all its sophisticated logistics are put to the service of brutal offensives. Against the powers that be. Caught between the Marxists *guérilleros* in the drug dealers' pay and the paramilitary militia of the far Right, the Colombians went out and voted, en masse, "Por La Paz," for peace. In Barranquilla, on the Caribbean coast, the polling stations closed their doors at 4:00PM to prevent any incidents. A priest, a slightly more conservative candidate than his challengers, found an ultra-contemporary way to get elected. He used hundreds of peasants, rounded up for the occasion, to inflate the already interminable lines forming in front of the schools and the clinics that had been transformed into electoral offices. Many local voters, already anxious about spending hours as standing targets for the enemies of the "electoral farce," gave up the idea of standing in the heat and humidity under the leaden sky. (In Colombia, lead comes from everywhere, from the stratosphere as well as from motorcycle gunmen, hired killers.

By what miracle did this monk (who was duly elected) manage to register legions of paupers in a region mostly populated by well-off citizens? By renting them cell phones, set up to make calls within the area. Thus, for a few hours, masses of illiterates were walking around with phone numbers in their shirts and trousers. The cell phone, that supreme nomadic object, was thus made the vehicle by which a wandering people was brought to roost in the service of corruption.

Modernity is used that way far more often than you think.

Nothing to Report

The street that was so noisy a few moments ago is sealed with a lead cover. The police sirens are silenced, their flashing lights are stilled. It is intermission. Everyone is waiting, quiet. Groups have formed. On the steps leading to their offices, employees survey the scene; tourists have put down their bags and are biding their time, here and there, and the soldiers have sat down. It is a rare moment. A moment of absolute calm. A pregnant pause. It is a parenthesis, relaxed yet terribly tense. For on a bench, all by itself, abandoned in the middle of everything, sat a bag. The safety patrols who have blocked the streets are putting away their portable telephones. In the absence of any information, they do the same as everyone else, talking softly, glancing to the left and right, waiting, smoking cigarettes, killing time.

A minute passes, then two, then five, then ten. The silence thickens. A paradoxical terror grips the city, stops the horn-blowing, herding the hubbub of the cars and buses outside the sanctuary, stopping fights, forging bonds between these boys and girls. A quarter of an hour. Nothing has moved. How long can it last? Are the bomb disposal experts on the way? People from here have experience, sad practice. Their apparent cool is a resigned, temporary indignation. The calm before the storm. What each one is brooding on, here, will be discharged later, elsewhere, in traffic jams, in the Knesset, in the pages of the newspapers where people insult each other, where people decompress, where people explode, where they ruin their reputation through scandals, scuffles and changes of mood. But that's tomorrow.

Silence.

Then she steps up, breathless, quaking. A girl, a giddy adolescent. She cuts through the line of soldiers that have been keeping the crowd away, and enters the plaza like a bull in the ring. She runs to the bench, leans down, picks up the bag and hides her face in it, ashamed, desperate, red with the embarrassment of being guilty of a military failure, a political mistake, an act of aggression against everyone. She holds her bag, upset. And the crowd, after a moment of uncertainty, as though punishing her and simultaneously comforting her, lets loose a salvo of applause. And while the pedestrians start walking again and the lines dissolve, while this united humanity breaks apart and returns to its camps, its trenches, its clans and its conflicts, while the lovers, the tourists, and the tired old men take their seats on the benches, the applause fades. Soon, nothing is left but a memory, the echo of this slap on the back, this way of saying, "You're a real jackass, but still, that's better than the alternative." In short, the memory was already faded of a moment of supreme intensity, in which nothing out of the ordinary actually occurred.

In Israel, there has been an explosion of portable phones. There isn't a single teenager who is not connected to his parents, his friends, and his school. Everywhere, telephones are dialed to warn and to inform, about attacks, massacres, the lists of those who are dead and alive. It's like telephone Russian roulette. With every ring, a blow to the heart.

At the other end of the world, on virgin territory, the President of Kalmykia, Kirkan Iliumdzhinov, a great beneficiary of the process of de-Bolshevization, also got himself elected as president of his Autonomous Republic in the steppes, by telephone. He ran on a platform including the restoration of Buddhism, the dissolution of the KGB, the abolition of the Soviets and the development of private property. Nothing wrong with all that. However, these are not the factors that won over the 300,000 breeders of horses and merino sheep. There was more: a Michael Jackson concert in Elista, the capital, and. . . a portable telephone for every shepherd. In these regions where communication is conducted first and foremost via voice and wind, where you'll get a sore throat trying to yell over the sound of trampling horseshoes, I saw with my own eyes, a processing plant for the white gold (the wool of the Kalmyk sheep) built by the Amalric company, headquartered in Mazamet, France, duly expedited by international contractors, new and yet rusting its way to a peaceful death. Modernity, one feels, is especially designed to facilitate the extortion of various subsidies. But still.

The call and voice messaging signals have seduced the survivors of a people whom the Red Guards (on Stalin's orders) had dispatched to Siberia. About a third of them died. And now, the fantasy of a flow of electronic impulses traverses the steppe like yesterday's red cavalry, evoked so well by Isaac Babel.

One last Colombian oddity. The 900-peso stamp, required for any postcard sent abroad, features a cell phone from Ericsson. Is this the magic of counter-publicity or a way to dissuade the writer from sending any more mail? It is so simple, a good phone call. . . .

The Symphony of Public Holidays

No offense intended, but Manolo N. does not have time to receive me. He urgently has to finish a case. Before January 21. January 21? That's a funny date. Maybe so, but for a Chinese man, a Malagasy, or a Kirghiz, it is a show-stopper. It's the new moon. A public holiday, a festival evening. Therefore Manolo N., back in his office on Flandrin Boulevard after the post-Christmas break, his stomach still a little heavy with frangipane, pays close attention to the quarters of the moon. That is the perverse effect of globalization. Draped in a thin layer of connectedness, scintillating in all its webs and other impalpable electronic garlands, modern commercial agitation takes on the aura of yesterday's pantheons, of astralism and idolatries. The honest tradesman who, in previous centuries, would deliver his little casks of hooch between two days off thanks to the Emperor, never imagined that one day his worthy successors would have to keep a calendar with them at all times, and keep track of not only Passover and Easter, but Ramadan, the Buddhist transfigurations and other occasions for family feasts. Globalization is built on an indispensable mastery of religious forms. The *New Age* that combines monotonous Buryat chants and solemn communion is not very far removed from the skilful trader who juggles the maelstrom of civil and religious breaks. There is no significant profit that does not require a sacrifice, an offering to the divinities of the diametrical opposites.

At every hour, at every moment, you have to be up to date.

Once there was a faith, Agitation.

The New Age wave, the cyclone. A brutal conglomerate of preachings and adolescent remedies. The *neo* copulates with the old prescriptions, wives' tales, and snake oil. A computerized trance.

While the Leftists were taking over college campuses, Timothy Leary, the hallucinogenic Pope, already understood that electronics and the computer would be the drugs of the years to come, that the "PC" would be the LSD of the 1990's. Faithful to his theory of disobedience, always on the fringes, he exhorted his troops to get connected and then take to the underground. His slogan? "Ignite and split."

The success of the 'Net proved he was right.

You can preach in the desert.

You are never alone.

The cartoonist Scott Adams created Dilbert, the hapless employee, as a celebration of the nerd, that pimply guy always riveted to his screen, misanthropic, asocial, sexually inhibited, and he coined the neologism *Nerdvana*. Elsewhere the "Nirvana" site is used by UNESCO; their screen takes the form of a mandala, a representation of the world.

Nuts

Don't be astonished by the new fads. The Agités of the calabash, prophets of the Blob and colonics. If the universe is going to spit in our faces, it will do it soon. As some of the *new-edge* groups have realized. Soon, they say, the earth will have as many inhabitants as the human brain has neurons. Then our planet, finally equipped with a conscience, will wake up. Already, the networks that enmesh it are like its synapses and nervous connections. The beast will come out of its coma.

Another *new-edge* suggestion. Whenever the TV reception fails, sit in front of the screen and stare at it. The frequency and the pulsating rhythm of the "snow" may be similar to those produced by other rituals: dervishes' dances, repetitions of Tibetan mantras, the stridence of prayer wheels. Let those candidates of contemplation not hesitate. Try it, as soon as possible. It's not expensive. And if the station implodes, don't count on the Dalai Lama but the television repairman. And repair to another room.

Footnotes

1. Faith Popcorn, *Clicking*, Editions de l'Homme, 1996.

2. *Loin de Byzance*, Fayard, p. 376. In the chapter entitled "One and a Half Rooms," Joseph Brodsky tells how the apartment that he and his family occupied, during siege of Leningrad, kept being subdivided to accommodate newcomers.

3. In May 1995, I published the following column in the magazine *On Architecture*, No 55: "Ready-Made. We all remember President François Mitterrand's famous statement: 'All great architecture is simple. Thus the square at La Defense, the pyramid at the Louvre, the sphere at La Villette, and the circle at the Bastille.' This leads me to make an even simpler observation: Take the François-Mitterrand Library. Turn it over, and it makes a table. Take the Arch and place it on top: you have a TV. Add the Opera de la Bastille and you have an ashtray. Fair, but what does that make of the Géode (a spherical building)? The kitchen trash can?"

4. Gilles Deleuze and Felix Guattari, *Rhizome*, Minuit.

5. "It seemed to be alive. It moved along the parquet floor about a foot of the ground; it moved away from him and disappeared at the other end of the office, under a curtain," in Sax Rohmer, *Dr. Fu Manchu*, 10/18, p. 137.

2.

The Agité in the Rat Race

Progress is an avalanche; if you don't move, you'll be buried. So the Agité moves, because everything around him is moving, and faster and faster.

The Agité follows the movements and sometimes anticipates them.

*   *
*   *

The Agité is Schizophrenic

Agités are not paranoid. They move, they escape. Paranoiacs are static. The boss, the bookkeeper, the CEO, born leaders, middle-class *compradors* — they all sit. But they are sitting in an ejector seat. Constantly threatened with being totally surrounded, they have to keep an eye on their escape routes. In the background. They will be sunk, eventually. Paranoiacs are always on board the *Titanic*.

Schizophrenics are too, but they don't realize it. There's too much to see, too many scents to inhale, friends to be found. They are particles, electrons. Publicity agents, organizers, nurses, sales reps, motorcycle cops, they travel and keep the world turning. They are go-betweens. Since they are alert to everything (for they have a keen sixth sense), they know, as soon as their bags have been strapped onto the pontoons, where the lifeboats are located. They already have sworn to themselves that, if the calm seas start to kick up, they will borrow one. Schizophrenics live by loans. They will sleep in a boat, under the awning, in the spray. Agités enjoy nature, every second of their existence. Agités are schizophrenic. They flee, they run, they fly, they hunt. Ubiquitous always. And they are charming. Where the boss and the assistant manager (the apprentice dictator) reign by fear and hierarchy (which is the same thing), "the schizo" uses his smile. The seducers are seduced by the world, powerful people are kept in power, under the world's power. The paranoiac also can smile, but it is the Khmer smile, the kind that doesn't mean a thing, a menace in the corner of the mouth that will swallow you like a snake. It is the boa constrictor's smile. The torpor of the Baobab trees.[1] The Agité is strong as a bear. You could curl up in his fur. He has a tambourine in his step; he is all muzzle and a bouncing gait. The schizophrenic often sells the bearskin before he has killed it.

To the great classifications by which we define our millennia (bipeds and reptiles, bourgeois and proletarians, Hellenics and Macedonians), let us add this modern duet, Paranoïacs and Schizophrenics. While the first may hold the reins of power, the latter quite simply reign — over the passing of time, over new ideas, over gestation. Entomologists of the airport lounge, they capture the age in its interstices. When the paranoiac, fired up for the attack, lowers his head and charges, leading his troops, the schizophrenic changes targets, switches his objectives, and goes after several at the same time. He's chasing rabbits, and needless to say, they often escape him. But he also represents several rabbits. He makes people wait, but he's already left, marooned in Brest or Litovsk. The ideal would be to go both ways, to steal from the other, from the Paranoid, the qualities that one has very little of. That would rub the ideas together, collect them, compact them. That would save the Agité from random dispersion, a tragic confusion, but his blood boils and his eyes grow dim. He sinks, disperses, spreads out. And the blank page darkens, while his blood thickens with black bile which, between you and me, is not a good sign.

"Will Jean-Jacques Debout finally sit down?"[2] [*Trans. note:* "Debout" means "Standing"] That joke is far more subtle than you might think. By suggesting that this second-rate singer give us a break, there is a hint that, upright, he somehow was holding the high ground. Seated, he would lose it. Really? Elsewhere an author noted, "I work at an intellectual trade; I work sitting down." Okay... All things considered, does power sit or stand? Is the sedentary position a sign of service or domination?

In the Bible, Christ only rests once,[3] when he stops near Jacob's well (John, 4:6). "Jesus, tired out by his trip, sat down by the well." This moment of relaxation was seen as an additional proof of his incarnation. Because he is tired, the divine is indeed human. The Augustinian interpretation gave this passage another meaning, far from the supposed humility of Christ. By sitting down, Christ indicated his power. For to sit down (*sessio*) is to take possession (*possessio*). And doctors have always made a habit of sitting, to emphasize their magisterial authority.

Where does the idea come from that, if sitting down is to possess, then whoever is on his feet (me, you, the butcher, the farmer, the laboratory assistant), is someone who has nothing? And furthermore, is it safe to say that a person who is upright, who does not possess anything, is "possessed"?

If the intellectual sits, does the walker become a manual laborer just because he uses his feet? And does he find, in travel, in wandering, in the dance of the dervish, that trance that possesses him so . . . magisterially?

In short, is Agitation a sign of sinking to a lower level?

In the age of globalization, when we are being globalized, when a simple laptop computers can be used as a control room from which one can, remotely and relentlessly, keep an eye on his employees as well as his businesses, does Épinal's contrast between the seated man and the upright man still make any sense? Franco, Mao, Milosevic, dictators standing at the microphone; Pinochet and Jaruzelski, dictators seated and moreover wearing dark glasses; the president of the United States standing to respond to journalists; upright autocrats, seated tyrants, people lying down. Am I still an intellectual if, far from the office, the notebooks and the calfskin briefcases, I travel the world? Or am I an intellectual chiefly because, in all the taxis, shuttles, trucks and fuselages that I use, I reconcile being seated with being in motion?

Does power reside, today, in the ability to be both seated and in motion?

In a strange echo of colonial imagery, the European pulled along by his native bearers in Turkish slippers or bare feet, in palanquins and sedan-chairs, the royal ride was enslaving, as is, today, the abandonment to which the traveler delivers himself once he has boarded a jumbo jet from Aeroflot, Air Africa or, worse yet, Burma Airways. An era that was ended has come back to haunt us. The backlash is a shock, for its message no longer has much to do with crinolines and fly swatters. Colonization has become very different since our strategists, high-ranking military men, realized that the earth was round. To understand the full implications, just consider that things that were just in front of you can now come up and get you from behind. Geometry, the science of distances, is no longer the only master.[4] Topology, the science of folds, of proximity, of rips and dissipative structures, has something say. To make itself heard, it types with its fist. As does the Agité, who wonders about his peregrinations, who peers with a little envy and some fear at the working man, the one who finds himself locked in a box of a building or office tower, torturing himself for no purpose. The planet isn't what it used to be. Nicely settled on the shoulders of Atlas, practically sitting on his back, now she is agitated, fidgeting and scratching as she tries to stand up. Her, too.

Michel Serres explains this, using the very apt parable of the handkerchief. On a map, two points are several inches apart. Actually, they are several thousand miles apart. But if you fold the map, or crumple it like a handkerchief and slip it into a pocket, the two points may be touching. The topological universe it is like that; it is the universe of networks, shortcuts, junctions, telescoping. A crumpled continuum loaded with potential. The more that happens and the more our world contracts, the more our life is played out inside a handkerchief. Is it our fault if the handkerchief is so often dirty?[5]

It's like the image of Switzerland, a tiny nation hewn with valleys and bristling with steep peaks. Take the trouble to press Switzerland with a steam iron, remove all the false wrinkles, unfold the Helvetian handkerchief and suddenly the country will once again look like more than one nation that is spread out and is letting go.

So Agitation wins them all. Even the most rigid. Look at how career promotion is handled among the modernized elites, the waltz of desk chairs and the assignment changes, which has now become commonplace for administrative officials, CEO's, publishers; it's a game musical chairs everywhere you go, a career roulette. The seats are all on casters, and give the paranoiac more to worry about.

Parenthesis. Tokyo is too cramped within its territory, it can't go on like this any more. The noose of suburbs, peripheral vampires. . . The city is choking, strangling. Don't panic. The experts have the solution: move the capital. They will set it up a little further away, plant it somewhere in a clearing without mountains or a river to limit it. In a plain, on a flat surface. Why not? Move everything. It's quite feasible. But is it useful? Other experts say that all of Tokyo, at least all that counts, the lists, banking information, indices, assets, codes, networks, symbols, amulets and cash-flow data. . . would fit into one suitcase. So let's move the suitcase. That's a ridiculous argument, a fleeting thought. Sit down, let's do a reality check. Answer one simple question. Just who do you suppose will take the risk of moving the suitcase? Who will take the risk of having it nipped, vulgarly, right off the railway platform, by some passing nomad?

A big headline in *Asahi Shimbun*: "Tokyo Has Been Stolen."

A Vuitton coup.

What mysterious inspiration led the design students of New Delhi, as familiar as they must be with proliferation, to suddenly start worrying about the uncontrolled multiplication of chairs? Adding up the rows of seats in movie theaters and concert halls, playhouses and conference centers, plus all the chairs in the offices, the kitchen stools, folding chairs, seats on trains and planes, bicycle saddles and even some tandems, they arrived at the amazing score of 22 seats per capita. Concerned with economy, these budding artists thus slaved away on a design for a folding, portable piece of furniture. Chair-umbrellas, chair-hats, chair-bags with a back support. . . Why didn't they consider simply squatting on their heels?

The demographic explosion that affects the Third World threatens our favorite armchair. It is not at all clear that our nice four-footed chair has won over the majority of the globe's populations. In Africa, Asia, Oceania, and South America, they continue to squat, when in Europe or North America we sit. Frankly, the aborigine's squatting position seems to be perfectly appropriate for a someone who. . . is on the move. The feet never leave the ground and their owner is ready to take off again after a flexible relaxation. The Law of the Jungle prevails, and being alert prohibits sinking into mushy mattresses and foam. You have to be ready to jump. Conversely, what we call sitting tailor-style or on the knees, traditional components of Asian meditation practices, are better suited to sedentary beings with unsteady spirits. Crushed by the seat (your other, natural, one), the feet fall asleep. Reduced circulation in the nether limbs causes a cephalic hyperemia, in other words a blood surge exacerbated by an increase in temperature, which can be very propitious to mental concentration as well as to perfecting one's respiratory techniques. Thus, crushing a calf, an ankle and some toes can lead to levitation. Oriental beatitudes. The faith of the yogi.

It's a strange planet in any case, where one fights for a seat at the Security Council in the name of endlessly uprooted populations from refugee camps. To chair a political committee is not a simple thing.

Moving Society

And for good reason. For "Go for it, kids!" has become the refrain of the great global din. If you take all the time that we think we waste on public transportation, on motorcycles, bikes, cars, taxis or airplanes, and add all the time spent waiting, all those interludes that fill our days as international Agités, the immobile lifestyle promised by the explosion of communications technology and video-presence is severely compromised. The reduction of roaming impinges on the dogma of a sedentary lifestyle garnished with remote controls. We have to compare the stereotypical hermit, happy to accept being cloistered at home under a tangle of satellite antennas, with the real picture of our ways. The whole world is within range of the antennas, but also of the nuclear reactors. That is the triumph of the *moving society*.

Admittedly, to agree with the philosopher Paul Virilio (otherwise known as the "cybernetic sentinel"), many of these are only used to drown the fish that we are in the gigantic turgid aquarium that our wave-covered planet has become. Still, relocating, even more than traveling, is our everyday fare, the air that we breathe, our aspiration. Some major American authors, like Paul Auster, Cormac McCarthy and Bret Easton Ellis, have been able to capture those moments of modern wandering that reveal our inner nature. The writer Richard Ford, the quintessence of the pioneer spirit deprived of its frontiers, summarizes this when he writes that at the wheel of his car he suddenly feels the desire to be the other person whom he sees, cooped up, like he is, in a vehicle that has been launched into the universe, looking for signs of life. Swing your partner on the macadam, with spirit, *tempo mobile*.

The Agité promotes the pulsation of the era everywhere he goes. He circulates, and thus revives the tradition of those monks who purified their spirits by exhausting themselves through walking. It happens, however, that in his headlong flight, bumps, ruts and potholes force him to take it slow. Hit the brakes. Rough road ahead.

Traffic Jams

Sometimes, from one parking lot to another, in the course of our peregrinations, our constant Agitation adds up to a lot of standing still. We try to get ahead, but we are marking time. This is the law of the traffic jam. You get stuck. However, it would be wrong to condemn it. A traffic jam is a rare moment of freedom. The solitary passenger nestled into a pile of metal, dozing in his airplane seat, has all the leisure in the world to sort out his thoughts. For the world measured by computer screens, he can substitute a world measured by the windshield or window. In the unfurling vacuum, his imagination takes wing, as though he were watching a movie. The art of motion, of movements, of trends, the world's mirror, cinema becomes a witness of suspended time, a reflection of the minutes and hours that pass, all uniform. Snuggled in, well-sheltered in the cabin, gazing out to the far horizon, the mind — under the influence of an accelerated production of beta waves — is more inclined toward to imagine, to invent. "After a quarter of an hour looking out the window," says an expert, "the brain reinitializes." Re-boot!

In this world of new arrivals, of direct access to the totality where "nothing is happening but there's a lot going on," (to quote Virilio again) the Asians got the gist immediately. Their movies are studded with timetables, connections, schedules, trains and solitary car rides. Wim Wenders was the first to sense it. His films, symbols of the 1980's, described a trend that we saw as an emblematic evil of the times. We were wrong. He went further. In his *Report on Clothes and Cities* (a homage to dressmaker Yoji Yamamoto), Wenders collected images of the endless interlacing of conurbations, linked the fluidity of fabrics to the fluidity of the suburbs, a silken anthem to the "Tokyo-ization" of the world, a long succession of megalopolises with tentacles wrapped around non-existent centers. Only video format could grasp this inextinguishable, continuous flow, and capture the narcotic shifts and mutations. Interminable long range perspectives recall Jean Renoir's musing, "The river was the first film." Today, even the *nouveaux riches* Muscovites, well-versed in Mafia connections, all sorts of trafficking and in settling accounts with a shot of Stolichnaya — or more likely, a shot to the back of the head with a vodka bottle, are in the know. The "M & M's," or *Molodye i Mobilnye*, the Young and Mobile, as we used to say — and the osmosis gives one pause — the Red Guard and the mobile guard, sweeping away yesterday's yuppies. This is the telescoping of the camcorder and the deliquescence of Communism. It is a burst of images or, as old Conan Doyle said, the surprises in *A Study in Red*.

"There's so much blood in *Pierrot the Mad*.

— Godard: "Not blood, just red . . ."[6]

The proliferation of red lights, lights intended to prevent the spilling of blood, doesn't change that. For the Agité, treading water is acceleration, all the same.

Mess Kits

In JFK Airport in New York, all kinds of fast-food outlets, "New York Deli," "International Kosher," "Combo Latino," "Plaza Gourmet" and "Serious Steak" offer to wrap their customers' orders, already tightly sealed in little plastic boats, in bags of the same material. The bags are inscribed, "Meal On The Move." In the land of movies, this is the trailer on the soup bowl.

Footnotes

1. Not a very graceful series of sentences but it's inevitable for, as Jacques Meunier writes, "the only place where a boa can find rest — and especially incognito — is in the baobab trees. . ." and further: ". . . Waiting for the Institute to finance a research trip to look investigate the critical topic: are there breadfruit trees in the Sandwich Islands?," in *Le Monocle de Joseph Conrad*, Petite Librairie Payot, p. 13.

2. In Pierre Antilogus and Philippe Trétiack, *Europe: peut-on vraiment faire confiance a des etrangers?*, Rivages, p. 14.

3. The remark is borrowed from an essay that changed my life, by Jean-Louis Chrétien, *De la fatigue, op. cit.*, p. 71.

4. The police understand this. Thus, Pierre Herbard wrote in 1958 in *La Ligne de force*: "It should be said that in the colonies, the first rickshaw that one takes is always pulled by a spy, an informer, a police stooge. . . . For although, in the metropolis, the police might run after you, in Indochina, they run in front, and you trail behind." (Gallimard)

5. I should add that the Agité, shattered by the change of time zones, jet-lag and the abrupt shifts of climate, is generally plagued with strong sinus colds. So he is very familiar with handkerchiefs.

6. *Cahiers du cinema*, No 171, October 1965.

3.

Nerves!

Burning the candle at both ends, the Agité takes note of sudden appearances, records the world's sudden jolts and society's fragmenting into increasingly restricted, mutually exclusive groups. More an adherent of the long term than of the moment that he captures, he knows that History will level, smooth over, erase from our memories what stands out for the moment.

To distinguish the event rather than the trend, to ride each new wave, that is what his instincts drive him toward. After being a seismograph, he plays ice-breaker and lightning rod.

A Motto

"Everything is governed by lightning." (Heracleitus.)

A Threat

"Lightning is the shape of a choleric corkscrew." (Ramón Gómez de la Serna.)

A Style

"I'd rather be a lightning rod than a seismograph." (Tom Wolfe in *Acid Test*.)

Don't be the one taking notes, recording, narrating. Forget about the after-effect, go for the moment; take the full brunt, in your face; let it punch you, pierce you, puncture you, penetrate you. Like a big receiver, a statue of the Commander, the "chief conductor." All vibrating with electricity, impulses. Fire everywhere. There is genius in a lightning bolt.

Events

Prigogine notes that, to define anything as an evolution, three minimal requirements must be satisfied: the event, its irreversibility, and its coherence. But what is an event? What separates *Before* and *After*. That's a crucial definition, now that grasping an event has become such a decisive mark of modernity.

Being able to synthesize things that appear to be unrelated and sometimes even in opposition, that is the first great benefit of a good agitated mind. To connect processes that, instead of confirming each other, seem to contradict each other; to understand that they in fact serve as reciprocal indices. Parallelisms, coincidences, synchronisms, simultaneities, echoes, the resonance of signs — every time, the event can "tie in sheaf the scattered significances," (Pierre Nora).

In the best case, these punctures will turn into telescopings. In the worst something, it doesn't matter what, will drown in its formless sauce the intuitions without a future. The event is a mark in time; a stigmata. The ability to decipher the breaks, the ruptures, the twists, the trends, is a skill that we now have to use twenty times a day. Be future-oriented, that is the rule. Roland Barthes already heralded the modern West's passion for ruptures, highly preferred over (duller) continuity. Thus our enthusiasm for mountains and our scorn for the plains. Soon, he wrote, all the tour guides will have to say is, "tunnel" and we'll all come running.[1]

To live in a permanent big-bang, that's the post-modern ideal.

Agités stay cool. They aren't easily deceived. They know they are subject to the requirement to keep up to date. They know they are condemned to experience the excesses of fashion trends, cascades of false changes, flashes of light that disappear as quickly they appear. A good lightning bolt blinds for longer than it illuminates. The trap is in the viscosity of the immediate.

For example, the stated desire to be constantly discovering new trends, to catch the wave, to be "hot." That's OK for awhile, then it breaks down. For lack of air. After "the neo," the neo-babas, and the neo-modern, then the "posts": post-babas, post-modern; then come the societal pseudo-movements that people call the "afters": after-modern, after-DJ-culture, After-squats.[2] Heavy. Our search for innovation confines us to debility. This proclaimed "After" tries to make the least hiccup into a Prigoginian event. An error of the rear-guard. "After" is an interface that has no thickness, not even virtual. It's a sign that lacks any anchor, the chaotic consequence of a world where "history" is personified, governed by the news and current events.[3] Running into the wall of time induces a backlash, a great retreat. "Times that have no *avant-gardes* are fertile rear-guards."

The old bag, the backpack. "After," and then nothing more. There is no more after to the Saint-Germain des Afters. And that's nothing new — weren't the 90's just the 60's in reverse?

The Agité must also shake the coconut tree of dreams, and knock down some already over-ripened fruits. The expiration date of trends does not give us time to ask for seconds.

Tribes

The proliferation of micro-trends is a ridiculous phenomenon, an attitude linked to our era. Douglas Coupland got it right in his caption "Musical Hair Cuts in double four-time."[4] Even so, tribalization is a real phenomenon. Communitarianism and sub-groups are disintegrating the social body. Free yourself from the others with a pulverizing violence. But any gap in the social fabric is a tear. Marshall McLuhan already showed that the "global village," by depriving humans of their bodily reality, by incorporating them all into an abstract mass, by signaling the extinction of the individual in favor of an ensemble permanently connected to the whole world, would drive them to violence. Once the identity is lost, it has to be sought at its limits, at the extremes. The violence of crowd of the computer era is induced by this tribalism generated by the global village. In the need to find a semblance of an identity, to redefine oneself, every one is tempted to cause an explosion. Overstep the boundaries, cheat, in order to be able to define yourself. Violence is a consequence of our disappearing. Electronic agitation has as a corollary the agitation of gangs, the brutality of the crowd. Agités, when they find themselves in contact with these pulverizations, must remain stoical. Through hard discipline, they use classical forms to report on the modern-day failings. When they succeed, the Agités can claim to have perfected a new form of eclecticism.

"In America, only 17% of the workforce is employed in the manufacturing sector; in 1980, it was 20%." Agités don't know quite what to make of this type of information, but they worry about it just the same.

The tribalization effect. Silent movies were universal; they crossed cultural boundaries. With the addition of sound, cinema gave in to the particularism of languages; it began to contribute to isolation, instead of federation. The art of movement, the esthetics of disappearance (as painting had been that of appearances) fractured the great family of viewers. The "Talkies" became opaque for the majority. An illusion of the image. It's not for nothing that the projector, when it was created in the 17th century, was initially called the "lantern of fear."

Hooligans

Moving society again. Fractionization and speed are increasing in tandem. They are mutually reinforcing. Everyplace where the environment is becoming standardized, the phenomenon of resistance is occurring, and dissidence is thriving. They are gaining ground, even winning. At the Park of Princes soccer stadium in Paris, they have given up pursuing neo-Nazi soccer fans; they prefer to subtly thwart the manhunts that amuse the crowds in the stands. The burly security men are decked out in fluorescent windbreakers emblazoned "Steward." Given all the strikes that are strangling French airlines and public transportation, the Park will be soon the last place where such attendants provide their service. Let's have some order, there! Move along! Steward! Underlying the flattery of the title (we're overdoing it a little, to pass off a police-dog as a room-service employee), lurks the budding of the phenomenon that Paul Virilio heralded: the emergence, the rise — as they say about the old military bunkers that, reappearing in all their steel-reinforced concrete, are emerging cockeyed out of the sands of the Normandy coast — of the "trajective," a concept of movement, somewhere between the objective and the subjective. In a world where we are bombarded with "information," this "trajective" is a part of reality, its constant and omnipresent metamorphosis. While it does not imply physical displacement, it supposes reception. In fact, reception of the streams of beer and cigarette butts launched from the top of the stands toward the goalkeeper's cage on the "butt-heads'" (in other words "visitors'") side. The cage is thus both a screen and a target, the goal and the ballistics, the tragedy in the trajective. Generally the reception is poor, but it hits home. Right in the face. The trajective, the tragedy of the active (spectators) vs. the passive (organizers). But is there anything the sports officials can do about these spontaneous crowd movements, the desire to change channels, to switch to a different reality by a click of a button, the spasmodic desire to turn off the long-drawn-out sports confrontation on the playing field and shift to a direct shock, live, real-time, a single play, sudden death? A shot that returns a pallid sense of identity, as though they were under the lights of the morgue, to the fans who are reduced to particles and devoured in a crowd.

Choose Your Prosthesis

If the earth is no longer to be discovered, if the blank spots on the map are nothing but memories, then we have to latch onto what remains to us and still defies us: our body, right within hand's reach. A *terra incognita* to be colonized. We're on the way; with a flick of the lancet in the fat deposits, a little face-lift, liposuction and re-shaping of the bones.

In this consumer bonanza, how can we resist the overwhelming plethora of choices? We can't say everything and do everything all the time, much less choose our words, sculpt our figures, shape our personalities. To the debate between thesis and antithesis, we'd better add the prosthesis, a ready-made resolution to thorny questions.

Besides, soon everyone will decide what he wants to be in life and then choose from a catalogue whatever qualities will help him to fulfill on that. Far from the stimulants used by athletes, and all such illicit substances, he will draw from a self-serve pharmacopoeia of "drugs," the first generation of which is already showing up in our supermarkets. Knowing that we still can't have it all, tomorrow any more than we could yesterday, we will still have to choose, select, opt, in short exert a power over our own personalities and above all over our bodies. We'll have to choose to have one kind of mind, to the exclusion of others. The historian will choose to expand his memory, just like a vulgar "laptop." Professors will not longer be "first caliber" but 400 GB. Others, more physically oriented, will prefer to get a decathloner's body for some exploit that might win them lucrative media coverage. This vision, halfway between a Jules Verne story and a reality certified by Inserm and Microsoft, has already taken root in the latest research where the Commercial Court meets genetic engineering. In this environment, the traveler, the one who, in the literal sense, packs his bag with three pairs of socks and as many pants, who still refuses the *diktat* of the molecule miracle, the "open sesame" to the planet, is soon likely to seem outrageously tacky. The traveler who relies on his own natural strength alone, deriving his resources from a single genetic stock, will have the ratty appearance of a galley slave, worse than the participants in the Dakar road-rally. Tomorrow, the medicine-chest will be more like software. And don't be surprised if by chance a few viruses turn up. Explosive bugs, mutants disrupting the DNA. That's gonna hurt.

Mutant

The era of mutants. Total agitation. While Jean-Dominique Bauby was still head of *Paris Match*, he suggested we co-write an article on the "return of the mutants." We signed it together. Years later, victim of what we would learn to call a "Locked-In Syndrome," Jean-Dominique had to apply the word *mutant* to himself.

While he was still in the hospital, dictating with his left eyelid *The Diving-Bell and the Butterfly* and while I was writing this essay, (agitated, myself, with feelings of guilt, knowing he was lying motionless, disturbed on his behalf by the absurdity of my subject, compared to the state he was in), I came across this sentence written about a mutant, by Syners de Cadigan:

"He couldn't remember what it was like to have a body. . .

He wanted to howl with frustration, but howl with what?"

Nike, Reebok…

American orthopedists have noted that the immoderate use of sneakers has led to a significant widening of the sole of the foot among teenagers. Little by little, the foot takes on the form (while waiting for the size to follow suit) of a large pizza delivered at full speed to your door, still hot. This urban mutation, by generating a flattened base at the base of the citizenry, has directly inspired the fads of sail-boarding, in-line skates and all sorts of gliding sports. It is an incarnation of the prosthesis, an interface of rubber skin.

Obese

After years of growth, in which the Japanese have been mistaken for Batavians, experts agree that the human race has stopped getting taller. Nowadays, we are getting wider. The flood of fatties who pack Kentucky Fried Chicken and Taco Bell are thus not so much an excrescence but growth itself. In parallel with the ballooning of networks, the extension of virtual links, the human body is also looking to expand. As the obese person no longer knows where are the proper limits of his body, the average human being no longer knows where he is. The violence that Joe Blow exerts against the external world, seeking to find a limit, the obese person exerts it against his own interior most of all, against his entrails. When society is globalizing and swallowing up everything, in short, when it stops bothering with details, it goes for the gross.

Downsizing

We see again the same pendulum movement: an outward journey and a return, from gathering to extension, monopolizing, seizing, incorporating and then smashing, pulverizing, disjointing, dislocating. The elevator society, the yo-yo of mobility.

So it is with *downsizing,* the philosophy of reduction, which keeps on growing. "Less matter, more feeling," the designer Philippe Starck was already preaching ten years ago. The proponents of this trend of expurgation, in their hunt for the superfluous, in their desire to reduce everything that can be reduced — and to the greatest extent possible — are increasing in number. What they are going after: the proliferation of credit cards, two-car garages, ten brands of cornflakes, overflowing closets... Their protest movement has some logic. It is the flipside of a process that induces us to accumulation, which the example of eyeglasses will help us see clearly.

Once upon a time, everyone had a pair (if he needed them). For vision, or for the sun; sometimes both. Today, everything conspires to make this utilitarian utensil, this visionary tool, into a jewel. The same process is at work with the watch, which has become the object of an absurd and growing passion. Thus everyone finds himself collecting pairs of glasses, which have been reduced to the role of accessories, just like a brooch or a hat. The annual turnover for this profession has reached the heights of euphoria and spectacle merchants have become owners of football teams, a major sign of success.

That, in fact, is what is interesting in this business. While American citizens are practicing their *downsizing* techniques out of Leftist idealism, companies are doing the same thing for radically opposite reasons. In many industrial groups, it has been noted that when a unit that gets too big, it begins to lose its drive. Consequently, it is split, the company is "downsized." To allow the employs to know each other, share goals that everyone can understand, give the most dynamic workers adequate opportunity and enable them to earn money and understand why — that is the technique. Thus, what appeared from one perspective as a reaction against shameful materialism, turns out to be nothing but a way of encouraging the market. Richard Branson, petulant chairman of Virgin, has proven that this dynamics of fractionization can bear fruit. Scissiparity, segmenting, breaking apart and creating competition between groups that were allies yesterday — agitation always, the pugnacity of reduction. Reduction is what gives a good sauce its flavor.

Satellite Worker

The corporate drive toward schizogenesis does not always lead to isolation. Thus, as a result of telecommuting, Sohos are cropping up all over the world — "Small Office, Home Office." Having realized their power, Japanese "satellite" workers have decided to gather, to band together into a pressure group. Via networks, they remain in contact and are organized. Offices where they can meet are germinating and starting to proliferate. These are not offices where you can share the photocopier (every white-collar worker has his own fax-copier these days), but a room where you can meet your peers. A support, a place that is actually in the middle of nowhere. In Soho, if you like.

Sexes

Division, always division, the tide that bathes our era. The Agité, more than anyone else, is concerned about the differences between the sexes. And is sometimes encumbered by it. Of the two ways of describing the world (that which favors continuity and that which is based on discontinuities), a debate in which each side actually reinforces the other, Agités choose the latter, that of ruptures (which is also that of conflicts). He arms himself with difference, which is also disagreement. The contemplative person may be inclined to paint humanity as a sum of identical parts, of replicas with two arms, two legs and two ears, but the Agité prefers to emphasize the irreducible otherness by which men are dedicated to producing sperm while women produce blood and milk.

In *La Pureté dangereux*,[5] Bernard-Henri Lévy writes that to save politics, we should rediscover our sense of the tragic, in other words disagreement. Irreconcilable positions are necessary, for politics dies from consensus, a democratic virtue that has perverse effects, bringing not a panacea but poison.

Reduce, don't mix; federate, don't unify.

Intermingle rather than meld.

Climates, by André Maurois. The pocket-book edition from the 1950's. A very British cover. Heavy as velvet drapes. A family matter. Very vague memories. And a question: that of the equilibrium of couples. Should we live with someone like ourselves, or seek otherness at all cost? The solidity of the same, or the strength of alloys? Two ways of mixing.

Weather, Climate and Bile

In the olden days, they considered that an excess of hot bile made people mad, agitated, inclined to eroticism. Conversely, cold bile produced phlegmatic people. The ideal of moderation was temperance, the happy middle ground. The Agité, who cannot slow down his impulses of exoticism achieves this balance by alternating climates. Dissatisfied with the regular succession of the seasons, he needs the extremes: -50° C in Khabarovsk, +40° C in Shanghai, a wind that'll cut you in two in Montreal, a humid, relentless heat in Osaka or Mandalay. From one excess to the other, to discharge his juice, to render his sap, to calm himself with a regime of temperature changes. If this is not an option, under our moderate climate, a cold shower when it's boiling hot, a mud bath when it's freezing. Remedies for depression.

There is nothing more terrible than a nation where the

weather never changes. The constant, humid 30° of a Polynesian lagoon has made the locals lose any sense of a future. Every day is the same as the last. Why rush? Toward what? They say that Tahitians, Fijians, Samoans, and Tongas are highly susceptible to the temptation of suicide. The prospect of inevitably turquoise tides, the multicolored mob of fish laughing on the surface of the waves, the haze on the horizon that vanishes, to coalesce into a monsoon somewhere else, are just so many morbid incentives. The Agité needs waves. If not a typhoon.

Outdoor Sports

A store full of camping equipment sends the prospective shopper into a surrealist stupor. The items on display would dissuade a Green Beret from risking a trip to the countryside. Every windbreaker is a self-contained catastrophe warning, every item implies disaster. In the abyssal crypts lined with walls of hiking boots and polar sleeping bags, the choice of equipment is a threat, obvious as a compound fracture.

"*Hurricane*," "*cyclone*," "*tornado;*" among all these models with such premonitory names, which one should you choose? I think of the panic of the mountaineer, the rock climber, the alpinist suddenly realizing (as the furious wind tangles him, rolls him up in a bruised ball and dumps him at the foot of his nylon igloo) that he chose the wrong envelope, that he should have been securing the vents on a "Typhoon" and that he was parading around with a "Hurricane;" what a tourist!

A Professional

In his own way, Jack Siler is a cop. Of the slyest and subtlest kind, the savviest of the species. On his own initiative, in his own time, with measured gestures, he analyzes electric circuits, dissects the skeins of power cords, examines fuses under his magnifying glass. Listening only to his own courage, his toes clenched inside his Paraboots at all times, he climbs on roofs, collects samples, scrapings, and odds and ends in his backpack, questions people (with his feet on the desk in front of him), takes notes, cuts through the most iron-clad alibis. Officially speaking, Jack Siler is an insurance expert. Not the mutual insurance company kind! Traffic accidents, car crashes, dental prostheses that fall apart (or houses, for that matter) are not his bailiwick. His specialty is the tornado, the typhoon, the Hollywood-scale catastrophe, the superstar fire. For him to move, to leave his spacious, elegant apartment in Paris, a tidal wave must have hit an entire state, it must have, in its exemplary indifference, wrought ruin and woe in its wake. Then, yes, Jack puts down his pen, drops his latest screenplay (he is the author of the best-sellers *Fire, Tornado* and *In Icy Hell*), and moves as fast as his short little legs will carry him toward the US Air departure gate.

In Houston, Austin, Miami, St. Louis, Memphis or Reno, Jack is always at home. The hotel always holds a corner room for him with a panoramic picture window looking out on the hovering menace and its panicked prey. He has no trouble checking in. The city is deserted, the hotels empty. Only the pro's, the wielders of wire-cutters elected by the emergency services, are on the prowl. 24 hours before it hits (and that's the minimum), Jack enters his cell. He turns on the lights, the television that is pouring out a loop of alarmist messages, and gets ready. Then, sluicing down a succession of cool drinks, he waits. In front of the murky sky whose muscular clouds are shifting from blue-green to ultraviolet anthracite, he waits in the city's silence while, bumper to bumper, the residents are still trying to escape in their columns of vehicles. He waits until violence envelopes him, until he is in the center of the centrifugal machine.

Jack Siler loves typhoons. He's been through so many that he's not sure anymore in how many cities he has barely avoided being drowned. One day, a ceiling light fell and left him with six stitches in his scalp; someplace else, his tibia was broken in a cafeteria. To tell the truth, there was no cafeteria left when this happened, nor restaurant, nor bar. . . only a great gaping view of the seashore, with abandoned Buicks and Subarus rolling in the waves, flying in and out of the lobby at full speed, as the hotel cracked here and shuddered there. . .

A shattering love story.

Love? When I say that, I think to myself, now they're going to want sex. How can we talk about Agitation without describing, at least once, the spasms and jolts, the wife-swapping parties, pleasure parties and the bodies of both parties? With all his mood swings and his need for variety, the Agité jumps from one bed to another, a little bit of a Don Juan, a premature ejaculator, a masturbator, a little bit of both, waving the Kama Sutra in one hand and a bottle in the other; he has every reason to sink under the gibes. It bothers me, it shocks me. This panoply of legs in the air, thrown in the reader's face, displeases me. Let everyone make an icon of his underpants. If he wants to. The sacred is everywhere. In the illicit interlude.

That reminds me of a successful English comedy: *No Sex Please, We Are British*. More than a thousand runs in London, ten years ago. It was a catastrophe. Nothing virtual, a titillating febrility. So yes, I prefer shutters and blinds, flashlights, discreet brothel sequences. Obviousness, showing off — some do it very well. They have an innate talent for what's wet. Not me. I'm not interested in their stories; so let's have mine!

Beyond a certain age, peace is an illusion. There is not a single street, not a single corner that can't conjure up a past that we'd like to forget, destroy, dissolve in the garbage truck of memories. Cunning stabs, a knife in the ribs, dizzying and cruel blows. Hateful soap operas, just as bad as those in the paperbacks, banal loves laid out for all to see, sordid sufferings on display, that is what is shown, that is what festers in these pages, flowering like leprosy, budding like a boil.

Because yesterday, while I was walking with one woman, I

met the Other; a third party, a distressing third, caught me by surprise. Like a monstrous wave, like a brick wall that breaks and crashes down, it smashed to pieces my very thin, weak armor. It is a nightmare, a bad dream. We are leaving a classroom, N and me. We go down one of those staircases recently repainted a ghoulish green. She is trying to outdistance me and while I chase her, I keep trying to dial, on my cell phone, a wrong number. I want to meet my parents (we live together, as a family, although I am old enough to marry).

N moves fast. On the ground floor, she slips into the ladies' room, a refuge. She escapes me. I would like to catch her, tell her, finally, that she is the one for me, she's the one whom I've always loved, whom I have lost so many times; but she runs away. And then everything is reversed. She stops running, she stares me in the face, asks me the question. I have to choose between her and this other woman: whom will I marry? Choose. The news fills me joy and — but why is this? — at the same time it paralyses me. Here I hesitate, I tergiversate, I handle it so badly that she takes off again, gives up on me, and this break, this frustration, this additional screw-up plunges me into the same horrible pangs that assaulted me before. Then everything accelerates, and I am going down an escalator in a supermarket. It's running at a crazy speed. The machine has gone mad, it's racing. It's going to break, for sure. This escalator is dangerous, it should be shut down, immediately, to warn the advancing customers. But it's too late. A man, a Black, accompanied by a little girl, steps on and both are thrown to the ground by the speed. They reach the bottom as if they were propelled. Then, what had to happen, happens. A woman in a red coat steps onto the top stair, and suddenly horror is upon her. Instead of following smoothly one after the other, the treads catch; they form a jaw, an iron wicket that grabs her. Her coat is sucked in, chewed; then her whole body rocks under the rammer of this insane mechanics. Then, not able to watch the moment when her body will burst under the metal, I turn away, I run away in turn. Then here I am back at the ladies' toilets. The Miracle Woman is there, flushed but safe and sound. "hey pulled you out of there!" And now everything is mixed up. In the big city, memories caught up with me; because one woman bumped me into another, a third showed up to set me back on my feet. That is vertigo, the abyss.

Folds of the Groin, Folds of the Ground

For days, we've been traveling toward the Grand Canyon. For days, we've been driving our Chrysler Le Baron toward the red pit. At night we camp in a motel, less than a mile from the park's entrance. On reconnaissance, we spend the evening wandering through the trappers' stores at the edge of the fault. It's pitch black. And madness strikes. It is 3:00AM and I sit on my bed, in the heart of the forest. I wanted to sleep but a dream has thrown me back into the ungovernable inferno of impulses. She was in my arms, she who left me without warning, abandoned me, dropped me, left. She cries, and our love is so powerful again that it is palpable. And I wake up on my mattress here, in an indescribable rage. I hardly know if it is just voices, thousands of them, that pulled me from my sleep. I hear them: words, complaints, cries, gasps of terror, chants, hammering, a whole earth fractured by songs and dances. They are the souls of the thousands of Indians whom the canyon has crushed, by whom it was nourished, fed, throughout the centuries. The tellurism is so powerful that it pulses like a volcano, assigning me the role of seismograph; on the page of my existence I, like an automaton, record its violent shocks. Then I see all the scars in the ground, all the faults that this canyon pulverizes and magnifies, all the broken women, quartered, streaming with blood, assassinated by drowning, cruelties, barbarities, panicked and possessed virgins. Then I know that, until I see with my own eyes the abyss that so disturbs me, until my eyes have domesticated what my irrational mind is building up, madness will rock me as the river rocked the canoes of John Wesley Powell.

The following day, in the dark of a threatening storm, the canyon is there. Majestic. Amber, all veined with mauve, green, fluorescent mists. Immense. Cold, aseptic, cleft. The terror begins to calm. Passions ebb, the torpor returns, soft, nonexistent. They move away, their faces disappear. Russet-red, ochre. Miles further, junctions, "trading-posts" in cities of dust, desertified, ossified: Flagstaff, Tuba City, Kaibito. . . And then, Monument Valley; and there, in this country where all the earth belonged to man, suddenly man belongs to the earth. Then, the flux decreases, everything calms down, eternity blows over me like a balm, and extinguishes me.

You're Over-Excited? That's Normal

I believe in innate Agitation. I have what it takes, in me. My family all understand that I must have fallen into some cocaine at birth. Since then, I burn it. My friend Michele Fitoussi, who is always crackling all over, claims that, while still in diapers, she fell into nitroglycerin. Very likely. She and I are two of a kind. We share the same hilarious history, ricocheting between Siberian frosts and the sunsets of Sidi-Bou-Saïd. The suitcase or the coffin. Some kind of survivors. Having seen so many bodies go up in smoke, we retain the irrepressible will to preserve our own. Not suicidal, not self-destructive. We respect the envelope we live in. We save our skins. We believe in keeping the wrapper intact. We may over-do things, we may floor the accelerator and burn out the engine, but our bodies will not be destroyed by chemical injection. Any more than they will be tattooed. Nothing will be wasted. Out of recognition of indebtedness, an investment, a conscience that is keenly aware of ascending thanks to our descent. My illiterate grandmother limped along with the long-hairs, the Sixties' protesters. A lesson. No moral judgment, no mystical reserve. Just a trunk that is consigned to you. The past, preserved, burns inside. Incandescence is its own fire poker. Our baptism initiates us to inexpressible memories, and from then on, we have within our frames, our bones, our muscles, in the depths of all our synapses and corpuscles, time to get caught up with, a battery; every stage is a booster rocket, and every age, too; an ungrateful boost, a stone boost. And of all the epithets that could be used on me, I like "booster" best.

In that second state, there is a position that suits the Agité even better than that of the whirling dervish, that cyclic fidgeter, he who turns the spit on which everything ends up roasting; it is that of the zealous vociferator — the howling dervish. These Tzars of the ziggurat, Masters of the minaret who bewitch the dancers, find that yelling satisfies their bursts of ecstatic osmosis. The hypnotic repetition of divine names, bombarded in percussion, spins the human tops into a trance. Meditation becomes fury. That suits me. I dream of turbulence.

What would I like to see, in this life? A bombshell pulverizing the Louvre! Yes. A fleeting shadow enlivens the sky with a streak of crimson, reflecting on the columns of Rivoli Street. The nonchalant pedestrians on the Passerelle des Arts don't notice a thing. And then, Boom! The neoclassical southern façade is obliterated, there's a great black hole in the gallery, a burst of pigment: Poussin at half-staff, Lorraine defenestrated, a couple of *quattrocentos* in the dust.

With a début like that, they understand what sort of person they are dealing with. Not the "office" type. And that's not all. Ask me if I have any regrets, and I answer: not having received the Medal of Hero of the Soviet Union! Just like that. When you stop to think about it, even cities received it! Moscow, for example. So?

Plus, I regret everything I didn't experience: the meeting with Livingstone, Big Bertha firing her shot. And everything that I'd still like to do, at least once in my life: throw open the prisons, shake the statues, throw a chair through the window of a tax auditor (I saw it done, once; it's great!), break every window in the city. And hup! Windshields, too. To obtain by royal decree, ukase and papal bull, the right (or, I say, the obligation) to rename the streets of the city. To do away with asinine names like "Avenue de France" and to rid neo-Paris of the dreaded aluminum François-Mitterrand Library; to choose instead the obscure, the abstruse, the menacing, the inept, to please Michaux, Mallet, Souvestre and Allain, Queneau, Franju, Melville. . . "Turn the Corner at the End Street," "Trip and Fall Street," "Avenue Street," which must not be confused (one is one-way) with "Street Avenue," nor even with "Venue Avenue," a cursed alley where one always falls down. One day, I fell flat on my face on the pavement of a sloping street in Bolivia, "calle de las Retamas." I remember it. I have the photograph. Everything is possible. And all those iconoclastic gestures, everything that one does not do. Slap a workman! Horrible! Inaccessible daydreams, hopes. Frustrations that ignite you, that fuel the reactor. And explode.

If I had the option of grafting onto myself any sort of appendage, a prosthesis taken from some animal or living meta-matter, I would choose an antenna. Others might choose a prehensile tail, a camel's hump to store extra food, or better still some telepathic sense; not me. Not the memory of the elephant, the longevity of the parrot, the speed of the jaguar — the Agité prefers the vibration of the subtle antenna. It is intrinsically a homing device, a social sniffer, a world-sensor, predictive and futurologist. The future attracts it. It feels, senses, guesses, suspects.

A man of lightning bolts, of shortcuts and telescopings, the Agité weaves ideas together, mixing and adulterating them. He is always on the lookout, on the unstable fringe that links him to animality. There is never a moment when he is not hunting, not launched on the trajectory.

In a text that was published some years ago, the art historian Hubert Damisch formulated, in connection with the painting of François Rouant, "the hypothesis that interweaving might, in the future, serve a purpose similar to that which was, for two or three centuries, filled by perspective."[6] That moment has come, and all of society is caught up in the generalized grid. To grasp it, you have to stitch it all around and pull. Now, it's not a pair of antennas we lack, but a parabolic.

Time for Your Check-up

Agités are not made, they are born. In a jolt. And then they simply are. They peddle their fidgets like a case of schnapps; an intoxicating heritage, a steamer trunk whose key must be around here, somewhere. Bruce Chatwin, a traveler-writer, hypothesizes that in his case, his turbulence stems from the Anglo-Saxon etymology of his own name, "chette-wynde," meaning something like "winding path."[7] Now, this is certainly not Peru, but it seems like it sometimes, and the Shining Path is already taking aim. If we are playing that game, then I am obliged to add, with a whinny, that my own first name must have determined my own mad romp through life, as clearly as a knout. Philippe, alias Philos Hippos, alias he who loves horses. (An overrated joy. My total ignorance of the world of equitation can only lead me to chaos and disaster, to hilarious and pathetic adventures in the saddle. So much for the name.)

Thence, this malevolent propensity to produce stones. The joy of renal crises, kidney stones, an area in which I am a certified expert, project foreman, delinquent. Gallop to stone-block. Montaigne rode across all of Europe on horseback, hoping that the jouncing course along rough roads would produce the prophylactic shock that would remove the accursed limestone conglomerate that was sealing his urethra. I have endured this hell. I know whereof I speak. I have experienced the frenzy of the internal convulsion.

One is not born to horses without being thrown, sooner or

later. That is the destiny of the stable. One of my more astute lady friends revealed to me one day that, as a prisoner of war her father, a French but Jewish soldier, had disguised his patronym Schwalberg as Chevalbert. This initiative saved his life, thereby making possible her own. Either grateful or unable to repay her debt, she continually reproduced that which she was trying to escape, by running around like a filly in heat.

And, if you'll allow me, once in awhile, to bear witness. After all the prefatory material, the body of the work. The root "Tri," which is the basis of my name, is shaped like a brace. In itself, it is pledge of solidity. The triangulation of beams, three-phase electric current, triumvirates, troikas, trinities, that's not bad. Of all the above, it is the three-phase current that obsesses me. I see it as the articulation, better yet the electrical connection block, of all this irrepressible energy boosting. Blood and fire in my very origin! So then, yes, the name! Do you think the long-distance traveler, traverser of oceans and of moth-eaten suburbs, should ignore that intimate territory that serves as his own anteroom, attic and monitoring device? Impossible. The Agité pulls himself together. He plays with anagrams, and searching within his own identity, he studies the branches of his family tree, looking for signs as though it were a roadmap. But it all gives him a headache. His name is a strange territory that lives in him and through which he is passing. A country to which he is seeking the entry code and the exit, at the same time, so he can flee it and forget it.

Logorrhea

"He talks, he talks as though he were afraid to stop." Terror of the final collapse. Just as the motorcyclist revs his engine and pushes his machine to the extreme so that he can feel, at the moment of acceleration, at the moment of the impending explosion, that he is alive, in flesh and blood and universal joints; and words come out like firing spark plugs, visas to go further, always a little further.

And there is something else.

To be Jewish is to be multiple. Simultaneism, fractionization. When a Jew stops talking, Philip Roth[8] says, another one inside him speaks up. Every Jew is inhabited by all the Jews. When the lay Jew completes his long-winded speech, the religious one inside him takes over. He wants to convince, to overcome this other self. To debate, fight, take apart his arguments. All of them, the Zionist, the Atheist, the Revolutionist, Kibbutznik, Refuznik, are one, and all of them parasite off each other, and I am just the same as them. All of them, at once, and several times over. "Two Jews, three opinions." Rather, let us say, one Jew, all possible opinions.[9] Irrepressible word, logorrhea, expectoration of the soul. All these facets, all these identities buffet, contradict, bump against each other in a desire to take over, in a desire for overall influence, a thirst for totality and survival. To be specific, not to forget anything. To begin again from scratch. Agitation of the thought, on the move. A trampling, a cerebral exodus. Neither insane nor stupid; the Agité is a crowd. A crowd at home. In the mind of the insane, there are rooms to rent, says a proverb. The antechambers of madness.

A dictionary definition of the Jew would be: an agitated people.

"It is characteristic of intelligent people," wrote F. Scott Fitzgerald, "to live with contradictions." Pretty astute. But nothing is more accepted than the idea that we should live in harmony with our ideas. How scornfully we condemn people who say one thing and do another. But isn't that the human condition and isn't it the grandeur of humanity to admit it? It's hard enough to have ideas; why should we have to take a position tht is considered to be "right" with respect to them? Nothing is more odious than the act that is committed in the name of supreme truths. That has always reflects some human manipulation, which Alain Finkielkraut showed[10] was characteristic of our 20th century. The tragedy of progress, which always suggests that we should make sacrifices in its name, to the days to come, to the future that sings with so much promise of humanity.

In this sense, Fitzgerald's words are the condemnation of all forms of terrorism. For, if you keep your eye upon the distant horizon, the near-at-hand becomes fuzzy, and the big picture is lost. Tension diverts attention. In *La Guerre est finie*, by Alain Resnais, we find this remarkable exchange: The character played by Yves Montand, who is describing the activities of his terrorist network, and a girl cannot keep herself from expressing her admiration: "Wow, really, you do very detailed work!" And Montand answers, "Yes, it is more the overall view that escapes us."

The terrorist is a victim of compartmental vision, of the detail. He believes that a step is an advance; a move forward, a move in the right direction. He mixes up the poles, he is disoriented. Because he rejects contradiction, he tends toward uniformity. (The terrorist is always in uniform.) His exaltation is the opposite of agitation. It is ossification.

Man makes himself only to demolish himself. A dervish proverb.

Footnotes

1. "In extreme cases, the guide will book be able to write coldly: The road becomes very picturesque (tunnels)," (Roland Barthes, *Mythologies*, Points Seuil, p. 122).

2. This expression was commonly used in *Nova Magazine*, especially the October 1997 issue.

3. Paul Virilio, *Cybermonde, la Politique du pire*, Textual, p. 57.

4. In his novel *Génération X* (10/18), Douglas Coupland includes under this heading the mania to subdivide categories of musical groups and to contrast them by points of detail. Bret Easton Ellis describes this attitude in his novel *American Psycho* (Points Le Seuil), when he reveals, under the pleasure that some people take in reading the technical notes of a multifunction videotape recorder or a washing machines with "28 programs" (each one more useless than the last), a morbid fascination, a desire to cut up the body parcelled out sexuality.

5. Grasset.

6. "La Peinture est un vrai trois," in Hubert Damisch, *Fenêtre yellow jaune cadmium*, Seuil, 1984.

7. Bruce Chatwin, *Le Chant des pistes*, Grasset.

8. Philip Roth, *Operation Shylock*, Gallimard.

9. Is Bernard-Henri Lévy doing anything different from that, in *Comédie* (Grasset), when he evokes *Bernard*, who takes on Bernard-Henri, when he develop his multiple "I," when he evokes again the double guardian angel of Gary-Ajar?

11. Alain Finkielkraut, *Humanité perdu*, Seuil.

Part Three

THE AGITÉ GOES ON THE ATTACK

1

Hair-Trigger Agitation

Melancholic, furious, a witness to everything, exalted, the Agité is first and foremost a revolutionary. From Albert London's "Iron in the wound" to Zola's indignation, not to mention the duty proclaimed by Dostoyevsky — to denounce, to resist.

"Agitate, never give in!" Now, there is a slogan for those who refuse to allow themselves to be burned by the spotlights of a society that judges by appearances.

* * *

Brimming with rage. But against what?

Tricolor Incarceration

Whereas doors should be opening to him, welcoming him, inviting him in, the French Agité meets brakes, obstacles, reservations and fatigue, everywhere he goes. He has to force his way through. He has to fight for every step forward. A sublime combat, for pathetic victories. Tables are set at the bistro, from 11:00AM onward, to serve lunch to the rabble: delivery men, truck drivers and the protesters who block their roads, strikers and the corporations that are locked out, nit-pickers, self-righteous vegetarians, pure and hard architects, as grey as their concrete. . . everywhere these weights wrap themselves around your ankles and restrain you, slow you down, persecute you. The France of slowness, always less; fewer cars, less work, less noise, less pleasure, less movement. A nation of thinkers.

Edgy Eric

A relentless drought in Agadès (Nigeria). Silence everywhere. Halfway to being a desert. Several yards away is a yellow dirt road. Shacks and piteous hovels, and further on, the deserted house of the Tuareg prince Mano Dayak, who disappeared when his jet exploded under suspicious circumstances. Hawkers, panhandlers, the tramps of the Sahel, prowlers seeking muddy ditches by the cactus.

It's 3:00PM. I sit with my back turned to the door, which squeaks and opens a razor's width onto the blinding furnace. Alone, eying my beer sweating in its glass, just 6 oz., hardly one gulp. Whatever you do, don't rush. Don't sweat. Just wait. Watch for this bronze day to draw to a close, eye on the mercury of the rickety Air Africa thermometer. Patience.

The door slams. An abrasive flash. Scratch. A Fulani, under his conical hat, with a dagger in his hand.

— Gimme a hundred francs.

The commercial ardor of frontier towns.

— Buddy, buy a knife. Gimme fifty francs. Help me out.

Silence. *Subirse como cerveza caliente,* feel your pressure rise like a hot beer, as the Dominicans say. It grows, it boils.

— Buy one.

Another one, the sixth or seventh, a blue cloud of djellabas that land on me like a wounded buffalo.

It's routine. They do not know that they are wasting their saliva.

Then, I feel everything crack, overflow, burst like a watermelon dropped on granite, like a carapace and mandibles bursting under your shoe. The mercury must have busted its glass, rolled across the table and escaped under the counter.

— Get the fuck out of here and leave me alone! I've had enough, *enough!* You're the sixth one to come in here and skin me with your knife. Even if you *give* it to me, I don't want any! You understand? You *got that?*

He steps back, disconcerted.

— But... But, I just got here!

Those were his last words, very judicious, very measured, very gentlemanly. After that I did not hear any more. He was right, but too late.

I was already outside in the open kiln, on the dusty ground

that puffed out under my steps and fell back down like ashes and rubble. I hurled myself out there as though I were trying to drown myself, I bolted, I paced, I perspired in the sun, coming and going like a tiger in a cage with bars of sand. A broken pendulum, zigzagging, staggering in circles, a ridiculous spectacle, colonial destruction. Since the last outrageous Paris-Dakar road rally, Agadès itself had not been through such vain agitation. Then, as though hit with a truncheon, under the flabbergasted gaze of my souvenir merchants (their eyes full of compassion for this Whitey who was coming unhinged), I backed through the door of the hotel and shut myself up in my room, under the airplane fan that drove away the lizards.

Agadès, one night later. I've barely set foot in the place, and the first greeting from a local, on a motorcycle, dressed in a short-sleeved shirt and plastic flip flops, calls out: "Good morning! Edgy Eric." And the swelling rumor accompanies me, from the hotel to the bazaar, the bazaar to the hotel. "Edgy Eric." The distracting oddball has conquered his parish. They may have gotten the first name wrong, but they were dead on as far as the adjective. Well done. Nothing to say. Edgy! From a distance of three thousand kilometers, they hit a bull's eye. Accuracy from the ends of the world, the scalpel of the native. A totem and taboo of nerves.

A Dreary Complaint

In the dreary Museum of Fine Arts in the dreary town of Rouen, in a dreary room hangs a dreary painting. The big picture called *Les Enervés de Jumièges*. Stretched out in a boat, the two tortured princes drift along the water's current. They were enervated, in the original sense; their nerves were destroyed. The Agité who is frustrated is that kind of tormented being, without volition, destroyed, punished for some fault that he does not remember but that haunts him. Until his nerves are completely shot.

Then Rebel

One would like to write a Treatise on Exasperation, to sum up our enervation. There is no lack of opportunity. Opportunity is everywhere you turn. Try any television or radio station, open a newspaper and, immediately: anger. Indignation at every step. TV news sprinkled with errors and misrepresentations, with blind acceptance of preconceived notions; diatribes that are repeated over and over, spat out left and right, anti-American or anti-French, condescending, hackneyed sentiments, from the Stalinist right, from the populists; feel your rage of disappointed love for yesterday's truths. Bristle at the lessons given by ministers, so prompt to accommodate themselves to the signatories of contracts that link us with those who gun us down. Politicians criticizing Israel, but mute when it comes to Syria, Congo, Serbia. . . French delegations running off to Baghdad. Rebel at the sight of France, broken down, collapsed, on the bench, on the sidelines, down at the heels, down at the mouth, 60 million somnolent citizens, invalids, semi-retireds, sour, stiff, petrified; old farts worried about their health!

Bridle at the a morbid fascination shown over the years for the troubled years, the dark years, wallowing in the Barbie trials, reparations, every side of the Jewish story, images and memories, the humiliations of the camps, Drancy, Warsaw, Papon, the ghetto, air raids and transit trains and repentances. . . Do these idiot lawyers, judges, priests and journalists know what the Jews have endured and what we others, the sons and grandsons, endure? Let them keep their litigation, their quarrels, in the background, let them buzz off and leave us in peace, let us go, forget us, close the book on this. They should stop trying to repair, erase, clean up all their filth, the shit and their misdeeds. They should stop accusing each other of having committed the unpardonable, while seeking pardon themselves. Too happy to have yet another opportunity to give in to humiliation. In this country, the Jews are welcome — as long as they remain victims. Let them become strong, and here comes the flood. People should worry instead about the Senegalese, or the American Indians; they should beat their breasts over Algeria, the curse on which they helped to establish by supporting the pimps there. The traces are washed away, but the scars remain. Memory is not an oil-cloth to wipe clean but a slate scratched with nails.

Take offense at the stupidity, the foolishness of the silly asses of the "right-thinking" Left, signing petitions, protesting on behalf of immigrants when they only know their upper crust, the last word among the jet-set in their moth-eaten sweaters and worn out shoes, a band of Colombian super models, screen-writers from Zaire, artists, scions of the families with the golden parachutes. Take offense at all those fellow travelers who refuse to register the children for school, anxious over the unhealthy living conditions of the immigrant kids whom one embraces in front of the TV cameras but whom one tries to avoid in real life, taking advantage of one's connections in the bureaucracy. It's indecent. Take offense at the white scarves of the socialist candidates, little princes of the rural provinces, war-mongering demi-mondains; take offense at the nasty faces, the hideous faces of the French fascists, mouths spewing, vomiting contempt for the top officers of the djebel and the rice plantations of defeat; take offense at the scant attention paid to innovations, new ideas, novelties, new trends. Take offense at the religion of the "neo," because it has already been considered, coded, targeted, controlled, registered, simplified, predigested! Take umbrage at the contempt in which this country holds failure, encouraging family management that avoids risk and thus avoids gaining experience. Take umbrage, take offense at the opprobrium cast on money, the sterile denunciations of the sour sociologists, the well-fed elite who spit and curse a non-existent pseudo-neo-liberalism; express your outrage at the trade unions that are riveted to their assets, providential societies for the already secure, blind to the misery of the excluded, deaf to the rage of the unemployed, designated gang leaders, mafioso of the red order, the black order, the ordinary order. Rage at your friends, your brother, your family, when they are weak-kneed, spineless; be outraged that it is stupidity rules the world, and rules it so badly; take umbrage at the mediocre, at the losers and failures whose aim is so good only when they are sniping at you; and take offense that this country that we used to love so dearly now makes us vomit. Be indignant at being obliged to be indignant, when one would so much have liked to be full of enthusiasm.

What is an exalted Brit? Does such a thing even exist? Did the nations receive identical quotas of subjects likely to inspire them to beatitudes? Can one even imagine an exalted Teuton who does not immediately take on the worrying features of Hitler on the tribune? They say the Malays are subject to running amok. A great foe of sarongs and paunches, he runs like greased lightning behind the sinuous sword that leads him. So they say. If the Englishman is an eccentric, a deviant but cynical dandy, the Frenchman is a revolutionary. He keeps quiet, blending in with the surroundings. He is patient, he ripens. And then it all comes out. Sooner or later, the day arrives when it is time to take one's hands out of one's pockets, to let the guns do the talking, to start the spring cleaning. And throats are cut, people are nabbed, people are arrested, people are thrown into prison, people are tried in kangaroo-courts in the ruckus that inspires a pyromaniac version of the *Marseillaise*.

This is the acute phase. It doesn't last. Just a flash. And

then the present disappears, and rancor settles in. The debates are dropped; the exalted one remains. He is not one of those condemned to the guillotines, nor a convention delegate in uniform, dressed up for the parade. Blood does not move him. He is not among those hordes of preachers and pedants, quick to give a prescription, quick to frown, to punish, religious bigots, catho's, protestants, frogs from *schul*, mohammedans. The exalted one stands to the side, he's quarrelling, in a bad temper with his nation, his country, his people, his fellow-citizens with their entrenched notions and prejudices. In a country where the proverbs encourage measure and restraint, where they set the calm pace suitable to asthmatics, where they invite you to keep your mouth shut and to adopt (everywhere and under all circumstances) the approach of a convalescent, simpering in his dressing room before a non-existent public, to nibble precious little sweets in tea salons where overheating is a remedy against vacuity, where an insipid vanilla odor helps one to forget the raging fires that are consuming the world, how can we hold back the rising fury?

"If you want to go far, take care of your mount," "a bird in the hand is worth two in the bush;" everywhere is this complacency, this acceptance of scarcity, this recommendation to avoid risk, to enjoy what little one has, Marshal Pétain's miraculous recipe, the art of working with leftovers, the anthology of the turnip. This substrate of popular wisdom is distressing. Take it easy, take it slow. . . We need the violence of François Nourissier's contrition; he called one of his books of *Forward, Calm and Straight*, to highlight under the calm exterior of the cavalier in the saddle the paroxysm that animates him. The exalted one does not go at a light trot. He has places to go, people to meet. The ongoing punishment, the constant reflux, bitter medicine, he leaves all that to those who subscribe to purgings. If he dared, he would use his nails to claw open some breaches in the French tricolor, crawl through the hatchways, and fill his lungs with fresh air.

In *Mass and Power*, Elias Canetti writes that the difference between the English and the French can be seen in the fact that the first stand upright in their pubs, all equal, to elbow to elbow, ready to face any adversity, while the French sit down in little groups, at little tables, and turn their backs on each other. That says it all.

Admittedly, mutual rejection is not limited to the hexagon of France. James Joyce wrote the bulk of his work while avoiding Ireland. He knew that a windy moor is not necessarily worth braving a firing squad. To all those who urged him to stand up and fight for independence, to choose the "Dubliners," Joyce retorted, "You can't change Ireland. Let's change the subject." People really resented him for that, and they still do. For some hotheads, that still obstructs their enjoyment of their Sunday Irish stew. The exalted Frenchman lacks the wisdom of Joyce. Ulysses doesn't dock at the French quays. Then, leave? OK, whereto? So, he stays and stews. He broods, he frets. Ah!

If only he were English. His temperament would overcome his languor.

Just one example. When London was being bombarded, shelled by the Reich's V-1's, Harrods was badly hit and damaged on all sides; it stood half in ruins, smoking on Knightsbridge. But it opened its doors as usual. The only acknowledgement was a large sign that greeted customers, saying, "A little more open than usual. Sales on every floor." It's things like that that help the English win wars. Can you imagine the director of a French department store, Galeries Lafayette, Printemps, or Samar, pinning up on his palisade a wry comment like that? In a moment he would be hounded, driven out by a horde of angry shareholders, all tight-assed, outraged by such an attack on morals and lack of respect for the dead.

One time, as soon as my plane landed on the tarmac at Sheremetyevo 2, Moscow's international airport, I was overwhelmed by the USSR's distinctive odor, a mixture of peat smoke, wood fires, poorly refined oil and exhaust fumes. Greasy gray pollution covered the tallow sky. What was already apparent, but in an insidious way, was that nothing in this universe of dirty snow and hazy horizon, was shining. All the paint was matt and the colors — a sad blue, dull yellow, rusted brown, faded greens — recalled our color schemes from the 1950's. Nothing was bright. One would have thought that some huge apparatus, an extinguisher of reflections, had turned down the dimmer switch all across the empire. Less light, less clarity for both objects and ideas, a general obscuration.

In the last few years, since the Union mutated into Russia, and Mafias wearing Versace suits[1] and riding in chauffeur-driven armored Mercedes transformed the entire country into an outpost of India with its all-powerful potentates and its processions of losers, it is France that seems to have the dimmer switch in place. For anyone who has set foot the same year in Shanghai (throwing itself headlong into the tempest of its leap forward), in Johannesburg (where a whole people is reviving in the pangs of centripetal criminality), in Seattle (drugged by its pure air, its limpid bay and its New Frontier computer ideology), France appears (or rather disappears) as what it is, a broken down country, worn out, growing old. The Agité is mired in the stagnation that tries to punish the liberal for supposed cannibalism, for devouring the have-nots, for class hatred. As though it were natural to prefer the agitation of part time jobs for minimum wage in the United States to the loneliness of those who have been abandoned by the system. But it's not. Here one goes under, and with no fanfare.

A Novel of the Rive Gauche

Exasperation. Some intellectuals seem never to have known greater suffering than a tepid champagne. Narrow-minded dandies whose entire universe is a terrace, history is a succession of cocktails, the world is one side of town, the Rive

Gauche. The trite music of their insipid love affairs. Novels written like chirpy little songs, frothy whipped cream cakes. Overflowing shelves. Weakness between the book covers.

Bobin, Pennac and Talking Heads

The grumbling grump, the fop sucking on his short pipe, the reflective one whose self-assured smile conveys more than a long speech, who, better yet, doesn't say a word but "is understood," so many self-righteous pains, jerks, turkeys. Humanity produces these annoying individuals the way a faucet spurts after the water has been cut off. It expels them right into our guts. They are in our way. And lately, they are proliferating. They have departed from their original status as confirmed bloody nuisances and have evolved into preachers of a gloomy new age. Their sentences, ponderous and slow, but stripped of the eroticism that enlivened Hardellet's prose, has glommed onto our culture the way tartar clings to the tooth. The Bobin-Delerm wave (popular, schmaltzy novelists) is an unstoppable landslide of prose.

Yesterday, we endured the thin-lipped scorn of the aristocrats upset at seeing France going down hill, today in their place we have some kind of retro imitation of their lofty tones, picked up by the Left. So many magazines have featured a certain successful author, a loudmouth who has taken it upon himself to stand up for the working-class, accompanied by a sheaf of photos by top photographers (Robert Doisneau, Pennac, Vautrin,

Picouly). . . the whole clique chimes in with their pet phrases and their nostalgia for the Paris of yesteryear, a kind of reactionary movement ostensibly in the name of the people. One last paean to the Soviet Union, and conducted by such prominent people that we hardly even take offense. This Leftist catechism, this humanitarian take on "Let's Build French" (like, "Buy American"), has a literary parallel among lesbian Catholics, who are really in a bind. The most striking example is still that of Susana Tamaro, a box-office star, whose limpid utterances such as "wherever you go, there you are," make the masses feel so comfortable. She certainly understands them. Pennac, in his haloed stature as a junior professor, has become the spokesman for a quitters' attitude that is now sold as though it were a form of heroism. "Don't want to read? Don't read." And to think that that now has the ring of some kind of admirable audacity! And we give way before this assault! No, one has to laugh at the courage of these talented "Profs" who dare to please the young while exonerating the uneducated at the same time.

Still, yes, of course, Daniel Pennac is talented. He is a peerless debater; he is admirable. Clear-sighted, quick, and just in denouncing those who criticize him: those on the Right, who accuse him of destroying the French language, and those on the Left who call him a demagogue. With all due respect to the professor, some of his courses bother me. Too much kindness in the gaze, too much Christian humility in the palaver. Too much kowtowing to the poor. Too many mugs of beer in place of ideals. The difference between morals and ethics? The moralizer always hopes that things will go on in the same state, so that he can continue his bazaar, promoting his morals over others'; the man of ethics wants it to stop. Two different styles.

But do we actually want that to change? That's the conundrum. While the Agité makes pretentious people laugh, the bore attracts attention. Bullshitters have a big audience. The bloody nuisances must not be completely inept! Oh well, right, sure, precisely, and the entire contemplative discourse carries within it this desire for renouncement that smears his entourage like the greasy smoke in a back-kitchen. "The less you talk," quips one of them, "the better you feel;" "What good is it to be agitated," says another, "seek within yourself, you will find the truth." Let's call it *Pravda* while we are at it. One person's truth will be another person's holy way. Cults are cropping up everywhere! Silence is golden, and all that.

To all these missionaries preaching an easy pace, the languor of the sunset, the setting of the sun on the horizon of our dreams, one would like to retort with some comforting, if disrespectful, sayings: "Vishnou la paix!" [a pun combining "Vishnu" and "leave us alone"] and "Ca soufi comme ca," ["Sufi" and "That's quite enough!"]. In Santo Domingo, at the edge of Las Terrenas, a local has painted on the boards of his shack: *Pensa antes de hablar* [think before you speak]. Quite right. That's even better than *Shut up!*

Always keep track of words, expressions. Never be satisfied with formulas. Get angry! Resist clichés and pet phrases.
Take the already cited but obsessive expressions, "a real rela-
tion," "real labor," "a real debate." As if there were fake labors,
fake relations. The mystique of assertion, the pedantry of the
ponderous style. Earlier, it was the expression "*au niveau
de*" [more or less "as far as"] that filled the air. Behind this exasperating turn of phrase lurks a dangerous semantic juggling act.
"As far as" is the death of the subject, it's general irresponsibil-
ity. "As far as pollution, things are getting worse" — a big blur.
It's not at all the same as saying, "cars are polluting more and
more," "the diesel is responsible," which is what one would like
to know.

We have to fight unceasingly, word by word; demand a
signature. Make style an offence, an offensive. Name the responsible parties. Never forget the motto of the Red Cross, borrowed from Dostoyevsky: "Everyone is responsible to everyone
else for everything." That's a bombshell. It's hard not to be hit
with the shrapnel. The Red Cross flag is a negative of the Swiss
flag, that streamer of neutrality or, as someone said, a white
cross. . . with a whole lot of blood all around it.

Don't be indignant, just understand that today's pirates are
only corsairs surfing on the marginalities paid by consortia and
combines. Technostructures and logistics. Fashionable rockers,

McQueen, Galliano, solo sailors. There's no security without wages. Subscribers to the false platforms, the Barfly and Buddha Bar, it's the end of rebellions since Andy Warhol pulverized everything. He sold his being even faster than his art, all his talent silk-screened, stolen, printed, published, mutilated. Requiem for the avant-garde. Cécile Guibert[2] points out that a computer can write from human voice dictation but confuses "dire" and "diarrhea," and cannot conjugate the verb "to prize," but has no problem with "price." The right thing at the wrong time, like the PRI, the Institutional Revolutionary Party of Mexico, the great corrupter, the successor to Latin-American Marxism. "Mexico is the Soviet Union with a majority of dissidents."[3] The era of the fake, everywhere you turn.

Fashion Shows

"He's in Milan, he's in Paris, he's just taking off for London, he'll be passing through again the next week, we just had him on the phone, he'll be calling back, can you call back? What was your name? What's your fax number? Cell phone? He can't see you this week, this week is out of the question, it's the collections, next week either, it's the Frankfurt show, he's on his way back from New York, he's in New York, he's in Milan, he was in Frankfurt, he'll be in Berlin, do you have e-mail? What was your name? So long, I'll remember you, remember to call back.."

It would be easier to interview the Rolling Stones and Yéti simultaneously than to try to meet a couturier. These creators of fashion are not people like us. They live between six capitals and spend all their time bouncing from one to the other, inspiring teams of peerless (and homosexual) designers with the touch of genius that will transform a bit of lifeless taffeta into such an inaccessible sumptuousness, so expensive that it will be a happening, an event unto itself. Fashion is to be seized, to be wrung like a rag full of dirty oil, out of arrogance, bombast and hot air.

Take the fashion shows, a pointless cyclical agitation that happens four times a year. Look at the fashion editors, and the envious crowds who pack themselves into the lobbies of all the smart hotels in Paris. One would pay dearly not to have to think about these kissy-face subalterns, but they, with their tans, supposed pillars of the "couture" shows, they make the rain pour and the sun shine. Ulcers are in the making, all alongside the podiums. God, how everyone hates each other in these factories of overdone caresses. At the Hotel Crillon, at the Carre du Louvre, in the inner rooms of night clubs transformed into chinchilla palaces, at the Barbès subway station, and better still in chic slaughterhouses, gymnasia reeking of sweat, it's all frills and flounces. Quarrels, attacks of nerves, scuffles among the photographers desperate to snap the ultimate picture summing up the "oversex" stereotype of an anorexic balanced on cockeyed platform-boots in pumpkin-colored sharkskin. Why can't they give us real Agitation, a little piece of India right in the midst of Paris, the amazement of a bazaar; why don't they give us the

Saint-Pierre market! Under the artificial lights of the prosceniums, bullets of hatred are exchanged, and rancor is cloaked in alpaca. It's no good! The sound of fabric rustling is actually the rumbling of catastrophe, of a flood of fire, a nylon tornado melting onto the poor world. A battery of sprinklers, under pressure; ah, if all that could only, with a good dose of watering, drown out the brothel of couture!

Had enough of all this artificiality? Of the profound philosophers of the operetta? They are everywhere, ubiquitous. As abundant as sand. Late one September, between the dunes of the Tenere, one of the harshest areas of the Sahara. Our Tuareg guide is firm. We must stop this exhausting drive into the great nowhere, and set up camp before night falls in the hollow. Praise God, Allah, Hussein, Husseini,[4] there are still opinions that do not tolerate any debate. Hit the gas a few times, hit the brakes, try not to hit yourself in the already straining kidneys, and we stop both Land Rovers. We have to treat them gently. We have rented them for the trifling sum of $5600 per week, from good old Mano Dayak, a rapacious trader, prince of his state, and for the time being, rudely dead. In the ocean of fine sand, we haul out our bottle of pastis, the only good idea we had while packing our bags in Paris. The sun begins to settle, low. It's a rare moment when the flies have gone off to torture someone else, someplace else.

Emmanuel Valentin, an excellent companion and skilled

photographer, jumps up. He turns and bends, takes measurements. He's fretting. Can't we move the vehicles? Position them on other side of the fire so that at the first light of dawn he can take a clichéd shot of the Land Rovers against the rising sun? While hardly revolutionary, the idea deserves to be considered. For a photographer, it is an academic case. Peering at the fire that had just been lit by Boubakar, our black factotum (naturally reduced to slavery by his Moorish bosses), the Tuareg shakes his head. I feel disappointment well up in my comrade. It is a fleeting impression, already giving way to exasperation. The meat smoking in the pan, the jolts of the ride, the total absence of perspective in this flat, dusty land where we are roaming, the frustrating sameness of the days, made worse by a ridiculously low hourly wage, the factitious joy (real, if one is an ethnologist) of discovering, at the end of eight hours of scrambling through the desert, one more notch on the local eternal nomad's wooden spoon, is already too much, but how can the pseudo-boss refuse to comply with the White Man who is working? "No," says the Tuareg, with finality. "If the wind picks up, the fire will get too close to the vehicles. And without vehicles. . ."

OK. We stay happy. We are baba cool. We lounge, watching the fire, the tires, the stars. It's all so "real." Valentin lies down, exhausted, convinced. Boubakar bends over his cooking pans and his thimbleful of semi-stagnated water and goes about his work. He is making bread in the shelter between the jeeps. Our photographic cliché is forgotten. We sink into an uncomfortable lethargy, waiting for the night to dry our sweat. We sip just a hint of pastis, for the bottom of the bottle, the last trace of civilization, is imminent. And sudden everything collapses. Our repose, and all our certainty. At the stroke of 7:00, the wind picks up. Panic in the dunes. The Tuareg was right. The wind is a frightening predator. Only this time, it's come up on the other side! Everything has to be re-arranged. The fire is blowing into the vehicles and the gusts are fanning the flames. The ground gives way under the tires and the Land Rover starts to list. Without a few quick maneuvers with the shovel, the roofs will be kissing the dunes, and the motors will turn to scrap metal. Forget about the bread, it's been ruined. The breeze mixed sand into the flour, making the batter into concrete. We dash about, cursing. If the Tuareg had agreed to the photographer's request, we would already be in good shape, but now we have to turn the camp around, change everything, and fast.

The caravans of dromedaries, the oasis at twilight, the slow swaying of a palm tree, the glimmer of a mirage. . . so many images, so many lies disseminated by vulgar cretins, fantasies promoted by those who put-putt around in the desert solitude of the city outskirts on their motor scooters. The customer of these factitious Paris-Dakars thinks that once the horde has been inhaled by the carnivorous dunes, the vast open spaces will return to their original calm. Bull. The desert is a capernaum. It is full of struggle, full of panic. You are attacked more often than you deserve. There is no territory that is more hostile, more shifting, more agitated than this great monochromic silence. A drama is always waiting to unfold, the terrain is waiting in ambush, a misstep lurks at every turn. Two dunes and a hollow, like the crease of a backside, a groin in the earth. He who ventures there risks never coming back. The sand is soft, the perspective is treacherous. One two-meter declivity hides ten others. Let's roll! For now, we have to deflate the tires in order to make any headway on the shifting sand, advancing at two miles an hour toward the retreating horizon that hides any asperity, that shakes you like dump truck on a roller coaster. And that is why cars up-end themselves and plant themselves in the sands like cacti. The serenity of the Sahara! Tell me another one.

Other times, other places. The Vatican. An echo chamber, a cavern of marble panels and columns, stucco and polished floors. At a fixed hour, in fact every quarter hour, when the tumult of the tourists, traveling in packs, becomes too unbearable, a recorded voice, a long-ago recorded voice now crackling and breaking, hushes the crowd. In ten languages, from the less fricative to the most desperately guttural, a resounding and unanswered "Silence!" clubs them over the head. Then, for just a moment, only the annoying trampling of the tour groups can be heard, as they file in to admire the magic of the frescoed ceilings in the Sistine Chapel. Michelangelo as a cowherd.

The experience is Disney-esque. And there is no plague to clear the corridors, no aristocratic Ghibellines to garrote the papist Guelphs. No, there's no miracle at the Vatican.

Another example? A Sunday in September at the mouths of Kantor, Montenegro. The sumptuousness of the gorges and defiles; negative altitude. Impregnable, ineffable. In the torpor of Cetinje, the forgotten former capital, is the false nonchalance of an intermission. A collage of ruined palaces in green and rose. "Montenegro," someone said, "is like Switzerland, only worse." "Here," says another, "war is slow-moving." Repose that is not restful, false contemplation, pistols in pockets, thugs' faces under fur hats. Cops in civilian clothing, between beers. Machine guns silent, under cover. A vertiginous withdrawal from the world. Motionless agitation. Danger tingling your nerves.

It Will Come Back

Basically, it's a fuselage. A white metal sausage, with a slap-dash new paint job, now the color of sand. Bland. The stench of kerosene struggles to overpower the odors from the kitchens. A kind of galley is positioned between the front compartment and the passengers. Who knows what they are preparing. Mashed manioc. The steward is impeccable. His uniform, worn smooth at the buttocks, shines like a reflecting pool. He watches over his sullen White passengers as they stow themselves and their gear, vainly trying to avoid the sweat that will eventually drown them. A lurch of the propellers. A shudder. In the yellow dust that blows across the track, two Blacks approach. They are dragging a folding bed, a bed frame and a mattress with squeaking springs. They are afraid the plane will take off, and they roll their eyes to make it wait for them. First, they try to get into the fuselage using the stairs to the cabin. Much shoulder-butting and cursing. No way. They slip in, with their thin bodies, but the bed cannot fit. Pushing, pulling, twisting. . . Disappointed, the duo goes back down the stairs. For a moment, the "expats" heading for Arlit, engineers in charge of uranium extraction, follow the fate of these desert comedians. Once they arrive, no one will be laughing anymore. Three months of dislodging the ore in this oasis at the mercy of a Libyan revolutionary *rezzou*, that really merits triple wages! They show up again at the front. They push their bed into the cockpit; they give up. Here they are on the other side. When they disappear, hidden by a wing, you can still see where they are because of the dust kicked up by their sandals. Finally, they're back. They have quietly made a hole in the side of the luggage compartment. In all dignity, they position themselves in the center aisle and hold on, their folding bed blocking the passage. They cling to it as if one of the depressed executives eying them was going to try, in a desperate maneuver, to take it away. The pilot crackles some warning through the microphone, assaulting the passengers seated closest to the speakers; the engine snorts, coughs, catches. The pedlars wedge themselves in. They bend their knees to keep their balance during the ascent, ballasted by their metal. The takeoff is abrupt. We go up steeply and the bed slowly slips toward the rear partition. The engineers are pale. The two Blacks are all business. The steward relaxes. Soon everyone gets sleepy. The two jokers remain on their feet for the whole trip, looking out over the ruddy glow of the desert. But they are the only ones traveling with a bed.

They could sleep.

Footnotes

1. Two Russians are crossing rue Saint-Honoré, both wearing the same Versace shirt. "Ivan," exclaims the first, "you bought the same Versace shirt! Wow! How much did you pay for it?" "$550," answers Ivan. "You fool!" Igor says. "You should have asked me. I know a store where it costs $650!"

2. Cecile Guilbert, *For Guy Debord*, Gallimard, p. 28.

3. Joani Hocquenghem in the magazine *Autrement*, "Mexico," No 18, 1986.

4. Gobineau uses this trilogy several times, in his *Nouvelles Asiatiques*, in an effort to restore the sense of the exotic. And we, in turn, will not resist the temptation.

Agitated in Every Sense

Agitation is an esthetics, a way of being, an art of living and a survival art. A proactive attitude that requires concentration within dispersion, intentionality within complacency, staying tuned in and plugged in, and constantly whipping up the horses. Shifts, marginality, changes of scale, asymmetry, dissonance, discord... every means of rocking the boat and of shaking oneself up. Let's look at the details.

Abusivism

At the end of 1997, France Information, which had, in its day, enlivened our waves, focused its self-promotion campaign on the well-worn topic (see our proverbs): "Too much of anything is bad." "Too much passion distorts information," "Too much imagination distorts information." With all due respect to the proponents of objectivity, subjectivity refreshes the world, enlightens it, gives it meaning. Once more, once too of-ten, I would be tempted to write, France keeps a low profile, strives for the happy middle ground; that "he who wants to travel far takes care of his mount." Information is tightly con-trolled, weighed against the promise of a pension fund. It's all the more exasperating in that among the positions taken, the views that are promoted, errors are legion. Let's admit that, on this matter, I militate in favor of "more," and even of "too much." "France Information, Information at a gallop;" that's a motto that would go the distance. Abusivist always.

Abusivism is a school, a daily practice. Counter Zen with pleasure. A desire to consume twice as much, to eat and drink with abandon. Abuse everything, and most of all oneself, rather than to abuse others.

We should make as much use of our freedom as we can. It is an essential precept: "He who exercises his freedom is not expending it but increasing it and reinforcing it." Malebranche. Art, too, with all its excesses and its transgressions, is a way of enlivening life. Abusivism is an art of living.

Rock'n'roll

I am snuggled on my sofa with the television on. The TV that I hate, as so many other weak-willed viewers hate it, hu-miliated. They are rebroadcasting the lousy concert from the inauguration of the lousy building built by the Chinese-American architect I. M. Pei in Cleveland, "The Rock' Roll Hall of Fame." The entire program lacks interest. And then Bruce Springsteen shows up, the great Bruce Springsteen; he brandishes his guitar and lets loose with his gravelly voice: "He doesn't play rock'n'roll. He IS rock'n'roll." And here comes Jerry Lee Lewis. An aging Dennis Hopper, stiff in his Boston prep-school blazer. He sits down, and only his hands are seen, circling, gliding, dancing over the keys. He is very good. Purely traditional. And then it happens. Suddenly. He stands up and abruptly sends his stool flying and, while he's at it, with the delicate hands of an artist he slams shut the lid of his grand piano, like the top of an old suitcase, all while making a perfect about-face that propels him in a state of disgust toward the wings, without a glance to the public nor even the musicians who play on, through inertia.

That's it, just what you are looking for when the virus of Agitation has infected you, just what you need, this slip, this explosive impulse. After that, you can turn off the TV.

He made my day.

OK, so should we take up the dissident's role, play devil's advocate, take part in the good old guerrilla politics of our adolescent years? In my great bazaar of Agitation, I was forgetting the *agitprop* of my youth. I left out the militant, the "differ" passing out pamphlets, the designer and the printer of our posters, the fresh spray paint of our revolts. A whole era. An ancient one. For here, and already long since, the politics of undermining have replaced the undermining of politics. The Leftist's tools are obsolete, the rigor of the militant is out of style. The spirit of revolution is completely gone. Nowadays, agitation is no longer in vogue with the public. A few years ago, FNAC [a books & music chain] tried to play on it by tacking onto its brochures the slogan, "FNAC: An Agitator since 1954." Agitator? Prestidigitator, maybe. The slogan did not catch on. It was removed from the promotional literature. To calm today's fears, unemployment, delinquency, AIDS. . . bravado isn't the right style anymore. The public wants a municipal watchman to maintain order, and preferably whole squads of them. Agitation is not in style.

In a sense, that's a relief. After all, in the ambient stagnation and rigor mortis of the Hexagon of France, in this country that every day shrivels a little more like an apple forgotten on a window sill, mottled with all its past, its summers, its suns, its harvests and finally rotten deep in its core, it is reassuring to find oneself in the minority. I know there's a risk of falling into the tempting attitude of the ghetto: "I am alone, therefore I must be right." The discipline of clarity is important. All the same, I want to remain on the barricades, to be avant-garde rather than a crossing guard. That's *esprit*. Agitation is still good for that. Get yourself out of the freezer. Don't go down the drain. Be international in order not to be depressed. And fight, preserve the pleasure of uncertainty. Yes, that above all, enjoy uncertainty, take the opacity of the times as a good thing. Build theories, sketch them out, ten, fifty, a hundred... Don't draw any conclusions to quickly; build unfinished works, overflowing, ramified, growing, freeform rather than structured. Keep striving for knowledge. (Freud saw this as an example of incompletion.) Always be groping, arms out, hands stretched open. Think, like the Italian art historian Federico Zeri, that the most fertile periods are always the first thirty years of a century and be delighted to be living through them now. Enjoy new ways of thinking, new ways of discussing, marginal thoughts, paradoxes and questions. Be optimistic despite everything, not about the future but about our perennial curiosity. Consider that the intellect, like a muscle, is steeled,[1] is sharpened with use. Don't forget; observe, take note of the quantities of things, indices, moods, suspicions, smiles. "A drama," said Alfred Hitchcock, "is just anybody's life, with the tedious moments removed." So sort them out. And remember especially that love is a work of art, an ongoing creation, to be rebuilt every day; it cannot be left alone, or else... like the apple in the window, like potato peels in the trash. Keep repeating that saying that never gets repeated enough (according to Louis-Ferdinand Céline), never believe that the game is over, that the facts are immutable. Acknowledge that nothing happens by itself, everything is affected by outside influences. Believe in that fidelity that guarantees us treason, perfidy, and disaster. Andre Malraux has a beautiful saying: "Anyone who was a communist will one day or another become a fascist, unless he has mixed loyalties." Use words, and books, to help keep yourself from despairing over other people, over all of humanity. Commit an act of indignation, of revolt, of presence, of faith. Enjoy those words that strike home, sentences like fists, explosions. Céline again, in the foreword to *Voyage* (and a sordid voyage it was): "I was born in a corseted belly. A bad start," Henri Calet *dixit*, and Angelo Ripellino's "the gymnastics of metaphors." Accept quotations for what they are, aids to thinking, crutches, a means of boxing the cerebral cortex. Adore, adulate the poetry of collisions, crumplings, and crashes, even silly nursery rhymes; haïku everywhere. Track every instance of absurdity, nonsense, the uncontrolled. On the 3-lane road leading from Rennes to St. Malo, lined with the warehouses of Atlas, Leather Center, Home Salon. . . you can spot this megalomaniacal inscription: "Rennes-St-Malo: The European Furniture Center." An immense talent for bombast.

Betray

And yet, betray. Shake up your ideas. Change your mind. Don't be satisfied with having one opinion. Look for the seed of an idea. Like this business of human cloning, the genome, the promise of indexing the genetic identity of every one of us. How can we, then, remain inflexible? Nietzche's aphorism, "Technique has become intentional technique," can now be applied as a warning. The sciences are cannibalizing each other, racing, racing toward the abyss. Of course. We all know the refrain: if such an experiment is possible, we should try it. You'll see. And then they continue, "If I don't do it, somebody else will, a Taiwanese, a Greek, a Moldovan!" Science without conscience is always in style. It's time we put a stop to it

However, doesn't that position (which, for now, has more to do with the Law than the laws), also deserve to be cast aside? What's interesting about any Law: if it should not be distorted, perverted, or ignored, shouldn't one sometimes, secretly, betray it? The terrorist who fights against democracy with the weapons of terrorism should be struck by terrorism. Without a stir, without fanfare, without media coverage. I never believed in the educational effects of the great lawsuits; Papon, Barbie *et al.* The twaddle of journalists, the circus of lawyers. Those guys, the less we see them, the better. The sooner they are eliminated, the sooner we can get things cleaned up. Wipe them up. They are tough, these filthy characters. Then, behind the door, that's what still works best. A bullet in the nape of the neck, in the wee hours; a cable car accident; a walk in the forest; without any claims made, no mention in the daily news. I am for an *omerta* of the State. We have to know how to betray. To make good use of treason. The State lie is a condition of the State's survival, as the lie is a condition of humanity. An attribute that differentiates it from the animals.[2]

Bestial cunning in Palermo. Italy. The Mafia has infiltrated all the administrative apparatuses so well that the "green" town council is actively promoting the development of polluting factories.

An error can be a flaw. Too bad.

In this will to organize the spirit of the era, in this will to domesticate the fortuitous, we make a savage plea for eclecticism. The Agité remains on alert, driven as always by his curiosity. The eclectic has this advantage over the specialist: his error is due only to ignorance. As he learns, he will only see more clearly.

The tragedy of the specialist: if he is wrong, he is often wrong about everything, and forever. A fundamental error, and everything that derives from it is off-base. Misplaced certainty only makes it worse.

An error of reason differs from an error of passion in that the first type relates to something that no one was sure about, while the second has to do with being mistaken on a point that everyone else understood.

A cruel example of the error of passion: loving someone who does not love you; and refusing to hear, when people try to tell you.

Go with the Fringes and Dissymmetry

Agitate, and never quit. Feel like you are in the right place only when you are in the thick of things. Move, evolve, reject the idea of immutability. Be on edge. Think how hard it is just to change your hairdo. Nothing is more difficult than to move your part from the left to the right. Get a different cut? Traumatic. Nerves and sweat. Failing to choose? Even worse. Symmetry, allowing the comb to smooth out the intervals between tufts of hair, gives you the glossy look of a waiter. Out of the question. So then, torture. The part is a dividing line, a border, a balance of forces. A trench that must be held. Or you're giving in.

Roger Caillois, in his treatise on dissymmetry, turns the knife in the wound.[3] Of all animals, he noted, man is the only one that is not ambidextrous. People have studied the contrarians, those left-handed pigs and weirdos, to refute this human peculiarity. A waste of time! They believed, in an enthusiasm born in the laboratory, that they had deduced through some experiment that a variety of monkeys was right-handed. Fire in the straw, or the bush. Dissertations were written on the tooth of the narwhal, on the twisted horn of the unicorn. . . nothing. Caillois deduced that asymmetry (and better yet, dissymmetry — asymmetry precedes symmetrical balance, when dissymmetry follows after a disruption) helped to explain the development of mankind. Dissymmetry is dynamic. It generates movement, whereas symmetry petrifies. That is what enchants the Agité. Playing on the seesaw, he runs like lightning and has a great time. He tips the scales. He puts all his weight into it. Conrad, in *Typhoon*, shows us a whole crew, off-balance for 200 pages. Force ten! When the ground is slipping out from under you, you don't express yourself the same as when you are in a confessional.

Seismic Mexico

It would be reassuring to think that it was just a gang of people knocking against the door, trying to burst into my room. A *mariachi* band, loaded with tequila as well as with grenades, determined to throw bags, boxes and customers to the floor. But, no. The guitars are put away, the sombreros have been stowed. It is the headboard that is knocking against the wall, the mirror that is shaking, the TV that is rocking. The shaking panes are trying to get free of the aluminum window frame, just like my stomach which has tensed up and is playing *Paloma*.

When you go to Mexico City, you hear about it, you worry about it, you wait for it and then, suddenly, there it is, chilling, overwhelming. The jolt, the seism, the earthquake.

I crossed the room in a bound, obsessed by the brilliant idea I had had the day before, when I asked to be transferred from a ground floor room with no view to this room on the sixth floor, facing south. This sixth cursed floor, which one feels certain will be the first to collapse, to fold up and disappear, welding the floors and ceilings with a kiss of Judas. A crushed tube of mustard, a vein of minerals oozing osseous flesh. Already in the corridor, pants around his ankles and the devil in his head, my traveling companion is dancing Saint Vitus's dance, trying to get his feet into his jeans so he can run. And then nothing more. A heavy silence. Dust. Not a sound, not a whisper. A car slows down to avoid some rubble falling from who knows where, and the barking of dogs harmonizes with the sirens. The enigmatic heavy silence of an irradiated city. There's no visible evidence, only the memory, negligible and already fading, of having touched the hand of the grim reaper.

Tomorrow this jolt, permanently imprinted in my neural circuits, merits just three lines in *Jornada*. It's paltry in terms of measurements, 5.2 on the Richter scale, a joke. Compared to the 20,000 who died on September 15, 1979, how can you complain?

Michel Onfray published *The Desire to Be a Volcano*. Yeah, maybe.

Mexico City: crime, earthquakes, overflowing sewers, sirens, factories, corruption, redemption, slow death, brutality, corrupt police, gangs on patrol, rackets, an apocalypse at every intersection and landing strip, open trenches in the shantytowns, fog, smog, pollution; from mid-morning to late afternoon, whatever you do, don't run, go slowly, moisten your lips and eyelids, take out your lenses, do everything to cry. Keep the children away, no class today, nor tomorrow, no sports. Diplomatic posts? Two years maximum. Afterwards, an obligatory re-assignment to the mountains, for a fresh-air cure. Mexico City the sick, Mexico City the chemistry laboratory, Mexico City loco, Mexico City the laboratory of chaos. It's a whole program, a promise. Go there as soon as possible. Check it out.

Changes of Scale

The Agité pleads for dissymmetry. The Agité is not centered. He is excentric. Marginal. "Life exists only in the margins," Balzac wrote. "Being in the margin," said Jean-Luc Godard, "I went off the page."[4] Difference is a dangerous game; it's flirting with disaster. A total bore when he is filming (he used to direct), Godard excels when he is at the helm. To tell the truth, he handles literary focal distances better than lenses. He has a consummate talent for changes of scale that makes him a closer peer to the architects, the good ones. Agitation, agility. Agility of the eye, reinventing perspectives and a multiple vision in which he builds his unique expression, layer upon layer. An outraged woman spectator asked, "When are you going to stop answering the questions obliquely?" He retorted, "But, Miss, if I answered them earlier. . . you would not still be thinking about the questions." Coluche did the same, juggling with planes. "I do not understand why people are such great fans of tennis. Tennis is like ping pong, except that the players are on the table."

Never to remain on the same plane, being able to extract oneself from flatness is an asset for modernity. Anyone who knows how to change his point of view achieves prowess. He can climb walls, walk on ceilings. Virtual ones, of course. The Agité must be that way, sliding from one pole to another, adopting the overhead perspective, or the bird's eye view.

My head facing backwards, my feet against the wall, my head against the wall and my legs by my neck, my eye riveted to the horizon. . . I am sensitive to poles. Nothing to be done about that. The "axis powers" have an effect on me that I constantly corrupt in my new starts. The loss of reference marks, and searches for refuge, too. An aphorism from Vicente Huidobro: "The four cardinal points are really three: South is North." The hypnosis of the vacuum.

Leaving. It's a way of reactivating the opposition between the nomads and the sedentaries, of achieving the great distance between roots and cosmopolitanism. Nicolas Bouvier refers to the frenzy that once seized the entire Swiss people, no one knows why, to suddenly escape the distressing verticality of their alpine panorama. He quotes, in support of this recollection, the suspect case of "what certain sinologists called 'the Mongolian cauldron'." Periodically this cauldron, confined in a tiny territory between the rivers Orkon and Keroulen, overflows. Hordes of riders invade and devastate northern China. . . One day, without warning, they arm themselves and come down the mountain as if they had to escape at all costs the oppressive verticality and breathe the air of the plain; but after a quick visit they decide to turn back."[5] To flee, to leave, to abandon everything, to get an eyeful of horizon. To gain ground. The dervish is not excluded from this rule. Decked out with a voltmeter, a prisoner tied to the waves, he is its painful quintessence. His hallucinatory dance is also a desire to break free from his anchor. The desire to extract himself, while never being able to do so. That, perhaps, is what makes him giddy, puts us in a trance.

OK, I'll extract myself.

The extreme gravities of geographical superiorities. The crucifixion of the poles. To always be able to find your way; to perceive the whole earth at any moment. My passport records my size (since the Constituent Assembly has defined the meter as a ten millionth of the distance separating the pole from the equator) as a decimal fraction of the earth's dimensions. A descriptive geometry as long as the day. Under the measuring equipment, the taxidermy of the people.

The Swedes rank above us because they stand on our heads. *Idem* for the Englishmen who snub us from their pointy headland. We scorn those whose hair we comb with our soles, the Spaniards, who, themselves, spit on the Moroccans who (being singularly racist) don't exactly appreciate the Negroes. Just look at a map of the world to see who scorns whom. Only the equatorial reversal upsets the analysis — the inversion of the magnetic fields, the watershed crossed. On the other side, the ordinary Australian is higher than a wealthy Peruvian; the sweaty South African is loftier than the richest Burundi; the tie-wearing Bolivian is a hillbilly to the Chilean; the Botswani is an idiot to a resident of Joburg. On the other hand, the Eskimo, despite his higher perch, remains, perhaps because he is frozen, a negligible cold fish. The Texan in his stetson is a yokel in New York and a Brooklyn Jew is an asshole in Houston. The Agité is acutely aware of these planetary bizarrities. His head is a sphere, a panoramic compass, a cerebral buoy. Weightlessness weighs on him. He has an accentuated awareness of his position in space. He knows perfectly well where he is, not only compared to his dresser, his office, his street, two or three bridges in Paris and a few monuments, but also over the horizon to Tamanrasset, the Danube Delta, a certain decrepit bathroom in Jaipur, the warehouse for double basses at the Capitole in Toulouse. Admittedly, it is quite likely that all of this is only his impression, a self-congratulatory magic spell that a professional survey conducted by a battery of expert land-surveyors, inspectors and geometricians, would contradict on some points. Then the whole vision would break down. In his agitated mind, in his agitity, according to some obscure convolutions of the anecdotic cervical folds, all the avenues would mix together, blending into an opaque mayonnaise of buildings, people and customs. The *favelas* of Rio, the *ghats* of Quilon, the fishmongers of Santiago where the infamous *mariscos* let loose from their bituminous shells spoonfuls of insects that chirp when they are sprinkled, all that hullabaloo conflicting and mutually reinforcing in a metastasizing planetary salmagundi. Even so, this acute awareness of the world fixes the Agité on an axis in the same way that the dervish impales himself, with his palms turned outward, on the navel of the world. And thus, in a torpor, he transmutes from a camshaft cradled in oil into a weathervane, a beacon.

In just a few years' time, our mariner, so fond of technology, has hoisted the Argos beacon to the top of his list of idols. None of today's single-minded single-handed sailors, pursued as they are by hordes of satellite-spies, dares to head out over the waves without his GPS (Global Positioning System). Jason, on his ship *Argo* ("the swift") set off in search of the Golden Fleece, supported by his Argonauts. (Don Chaffey composed a breathless epic about this.) But his navigation equipment was damaged, and his boat veered off course. And so this compass, in complete disarray, its needle frenetically spinning one way and another under glass, is the symbol that has federated, over the centuries, all the Golden Fleeces: the ancient one, and the one that Leon Degrelle* tried to raise in 1942 — longitudes and latitudes confounded in the interlacing of history and geography.

I used to need a compass in order to find my apartment. How much time I wasted — I'd still be looking, if I hadn't got one. I have trouble getting my bearings. At the time, while I was exploring the halls, the elevators and the tiny apartments in various buildings, I used to carry one in my pocket. I would take it out, between two doors, in order to verify how much sunlight a room would get. In my youth, my buddies used to call me "The Compass." During a visit to Amsterdam, when the

* founder and leader of Belgium's pro-Nazi Rexist Party, and commander of the Walloon and Flemish storm-troopers that fought on the Russian front.

Boomstraat was a big thing and the freaks would sleep in a heap in the cargo compartment of a dealer's barge in exchange for a handful of guilders (the long-ago decade of the *Paradiso*, when you could come across lost souls who, for an hour of flipping out, incurred years of flashbacks), my pals were impressed by my skill in locating our refuge in the circular maze of Berlage. In the mists, I always managed to find the stairwell that we had named TB, or "temporary berth," which served as a refuge for drunken beatniks, which is what we were at the time.

Since then, I regard the sense of orientation as one of my crucial survival tools. It is a lifesaver. The sense of orientation is as essential to the Agité as the foghorn is to the *Flying Dutchman* or his trunk is to the elephant. A hand, an extra fist. And in a free-for-all, that can make a difference.

The Agité Shoots Off His Mouth

The language business is not rational. Language is a vehicle, and anyone who drives it recklessly should expect some problems.[6] Language is a greased skid. Slip, slide, stumble and lurch; trouble is lurking everywhere. The danger is in allowing yourself to get started, heading down a certain path, being led on by your tongue, losing your head. Language is a dominatrix. Perverse. It lets you be in control, then it bucks. Anyone riding the horse of language will find it hard to get down safely.

The Agité is very often brought to his knees by the wonder of his tongue. How can you resist it? Its range is so broad, its inventory so beautiful. To let oneself go, to give in to all the shifts in meaning, all the *doubles entendres*, all the opportunities to make a pun. To give in to the poetry of plays on words, to sit on the shoulder of Paolo Uccello as he bent in the pallid gleam of a candle over his complex problems of perspective, murmuring perfidiously to his wife when she called him to her bed: *"O, che dolce cosa é questa prospettiva!"* To always blaze, blazon, blasé in a blazer. . . And how about a new revolutionary cry: "Eradicate heraldics!" And then the most enigmatic, most beautiful, and most secret. Why is the negation of "eight" equivalent to the night? *Huit, nuit; otto, notte; ocho, noche; eight, night; acht, nacht.* "Eight" asleep and lying on its side is the symbol of infinity with a female silhouette. How can you not be struck by that?

And if a good laugh offers as many benefits as a good roll in the hay, how much beneficial must be a good roll in the "say"?

Agitation, exaltation, gesticulation, dissemination, indig-nation, so many terms are held within each other, a matryoshka of the palate, lexical logorrhea. All the precision of buckshot.

Going Off-Course

If you are always trying to do things differently, to follow a less obvious path, to climb the embankment at the steepest point, you end up falling down a lot. Motorcyclists know the gyroscopic effect that tries to pull you off the road when you are traveling at high speeds. No one tips a handlebar without risking a loss of balance, no one gets too friendly with the centrifuge with impunity. The faster you go, the greater the risk of being thrown. You are thrown off course.

Here is a term that is not very clear. Its meanings are jumbled. When you say "exaltation," psychoanalyst Juan David Nasio hears "exaction." Crime and delictus. ("Deli"?) Might one not also hear "ex-halt in Zion"? And how can we miss hearing, in this too strong "H," this "H" of exhaling, of exhalation, both breath and asphyxiation, asthmatic coercion, the tightening of the bronchi? I swore to myself. . . not to get mired in the past, the culture of exile. To make fun of it. To "play" travel-writer. But how often, throughout all these travels, on trails and trains, in hotels and motels, do we get this feeling that it's all just a rehearsal, a practice run? I'm ready for the big jump, the exodus, the stampede. To be, in my turn, a greenhorn, a tenderfoot, an immigrant. Something of the grandeur of the pioneer can be found in voluntary exile. There is audacity. There is an assault. And an insult, too. Like a spit on the back of your jacket. An affront that does not go away. Agitate in Zion. My Jerusalem. My Holy Sepulchre, my *via dolorosa*. One does what one can, with what one has.

Veering

Michel Pastoureau, a high-flying medievalist, author of a remarkable essay on stripes,[7] tackled the study of a history of pejorative codes in the West. After having dealt with the stripe and explored the dishonorable yellow, he took up zigzags, the syncopated step of the bewitched, the lame. Angelo Ripellino recalls, in his *Praga Magica* (published by Plon) that a furious King Rudolph, "walked diagonally."

In China (contrary to our societies), the devil goes straight while the healthy spirit zigzags. In Shanghai, this is the key to the city, that which makes opens doors and connects you a little more closely to the reality of this southernmost city, an Asian Marseilles, den of dark pleasures. In Beijing, a pitiless city of pitiless power, the avenues are cut at right angles. Sharp angles. Shanghai is all curves and the Shanghainese, who (thanks to their slitted dresses and a few concessions) have done so much for the reputation of their city, have curves that, on my honor as a specialist, the Pekinese do not have. The philosopher and si-nologist François Jullien, an eminent scrutinizer of the out-standing characteristics of the Celestial City, confirms it. As does an "expat" whom they have bewitched and who adds, "Shanghai women are thinner to look at than they are to touch." Zigzags, lameness, convolutions, twists and turns, so many mis-deeds of the intellect, celebrated in China, repudiated here.

The contribution of roundness, the power of advantages. "When you have followed Arabic writing with your eyes, you will understand the iron of Latin writing." The sensuality of interlacings. In truth, agitation is closely entwined with pen-manship. Each is a school of jubilation. The arabesque is an in-toxication. In Arabic as in Hebrew, only the consonants are noted. Writing is dry. Only the spoken word, which makes the vowels emerge, electrifies the text. In Arabic, the word for "vowel" is *araka*: "movement." Maybe this is where the spiral comes from, the Black Stone of the Kaaba, maintained like a fire since the 6th century, bringing forth the holy scripture from a cave in the desert, like a whirlwind. Aiding millions and millions of pilgrims, it unfolds like a parchment whose letters are beings and whose ink is a clamor. Yes, guide letters, female curves, biomorphism, the hypnosis of dervish music. At the "Imagination" exhibition in 1995, one of the exhibitors displayed a virtual erotic game entitled, "Is the Devil a Curve?"

Out and back, zigzags. Isn't that what counts, the subversive glance, the stolen moment? The Agité in his exaltation is taking advantage of all these openings. See without being seen, dig around in the baggage, look through the keyhole, spy on your mistress, spy on her lover, whatever seems good to you. Ah, the vicious one, the cavalier, the rider! How do you dismount from such a horse!

The Agité likes curves and convolutions. He goes ahead by jolts, by zigzags; he circumvents obstacles. He prefers tricks and turns over the force of attack. He turns around before sacking and pillaging. The Agité has more than one trick in his sack.

Don't Wait

Act fast, keep moving. Contemplation is heresy. Never let yourself get caught at a standstill. Everything moves, and accelerates. I had a distressing experience, actually it's a vulgar anecdote. Almost nothing. Eleven years ago, every day while I was in Jerusalem, I promised myself I'd buy a few pounds of Turkish delights in the Old City. Every day, I put it off. And then finally, there was a shooting on the Holy Mount, a soldier from Tsahal went mad and shot the Moslem faithful. Terror and strikes, iron curtains that fell like battle axes. Absolute silence. Good-bye, Turkish delights.

The slightest desire suddenly thwarted by backwardness, hatred, blood. Sweets sacrificed to bitterness. In the land of milk and honey. One more time.

Don't wait.

Sinking

In the ballistic society, on the highway of flaring destinies, lives are traced like tracer bullets. A flash, and then nothing. On the crown of the hood, the Mercedes symbol is a gun sight. The road is a launch pad, the destination a target, the car, a weapon. But nowadays, the gun rack is packed. Hunters are everywhere. Photographers, paparazzi, television viewers armed with remote controls.

Somewhere. Nigeria. All night the bus, heading through the humidity, the mud, the sweat, the decibels, has charged along the thousand kilometers of straight line connecting Agadès to Niamey. Day is breaking. The bus stops swaying and applies its brakes in the dust. Halt. I collapse on a pile of stones, sticky, stiff, bored. A young man walks up. He sits across from me.

"Now, we will converse."

Mysore of Mysore

A swirl of dust and dirty shirts; the end of a riot or, more likely, its moment of ignition. A return of the flame of slaughters, long massacres? In the background, beyond the rows of excited people who are congregating, between the cars that are packing the roadway and out of which spout drivers without shoes, hirsute and enlightened, one has to bust heads with blows of bamboo to drive the half-broken natives toward buses with broken axles. We have stopped. A thin metal balustrade isolates us from the crowd that ebbs and flows again, convulsing in the dry heat. An acrid odor of sweat mixed with burning rubber wafts over us in waves from the main street of Mysore. In the days before the monsoon, it is like the first breath of wind that stimulates the crowd that has been stupefied by months of discomfort. But over there, the rows are breaking, exploding under the blows of a tire iron. People are running, flying, racing; people rush toward us and in the mob that surrounds us I clutch a *dhoti* by the fringe to ask whether I need to flee, or pray.

–*Demonstration? Riots?*

–*No sir, No, No. Family problem!*

An Open Tomb

A famous racing driver says, "When you're going 300 miles per hour, surrounded by other racers, and suddenly, at the end of the straightway, at the beginning of the curve, you see a big mass of smoke. . . That's the time to hit the gas, because you know that instinctively all the others will lift their feet off the pedal."

A Closed Tomb

You can jump without a parachute, but you can only do it once. You can't make it a way of life.

India

It is a great prize, but it doesn't win you anything. At best, you don't lose. If you lose, such is life. People die, and often several at once, ten, fifteen, twenty deaths sometimes. If it's head-on. The rest of the time, it is a matter of ballistics, calculating the curve, keeping an eye on the escape route. Sound is enormously important. Blow your horn to clear a path. Then, swerve to the side, maneuver and wind your way through, veer off onto the shoulder, wave your hand out the window, warn, inform, dodge, avoid, evade, slam your foot on the brakes but keep moving, stay fluid. It is Indian roulette. The game is always on. Firing ranges, target practice everywhere.

Two accidents in five trips. The first on the way to Calcutta, with Dominique Lapierre and five others guys including one who was dying. We were going sixty when we were rammed by a motorcoach. The Ambassador was up on two wheels, reamed in the side, the frame was bent. Two wounded. No report filed. The second in Goa, around midnight, in a taxi. A straight road, and the engine floored. The sound of gears and pistons being flayed, torn and strangled and then the sudden swerve toward the middle, and dead-on, the big Enfield and the two Indians perched on the footrests of the motorcycle. A huge impact, smashing metal. No casualties. A lot of insults.

Cheating

Russian roulette. Try your luck. Take a risk. Cheat. Here and everywhere, look how everyone curses the referees. Feet up, in front of our television sets, ensconced in our designer living rooms, we have all the leisure in the world to comment on the mistakes made by these officials in shorts. Let a sweaty referee wrongly grant a penalty that kills the "visitors" and it's a free-for-all. The crowd jumps to its feet in a frenzy and calls for sanctions and, especially, recourse to modern techniques. Let's have an end to randomness, that shortcoming that keeps sports from becoming an exact science. The people demand a "replay!" And then there is the old trick of direct video monitoring. A tackle in the end zone and suddenly, in the linesman's headset, the truth spouts out of a TV camera located somewhere in the stands.

Compare this additional electronic intrusion of the all-holy image into an instance of jurisdiction, and the following worthy remark by a hockey player. Talking about the violent impacts, collisions at over sixty miles per hour with the Plexiglass walls around the rinks, he mischievously concludes, "Since it is strictly prohibited to use your stick to trip an adversary, the whole game consists in doing just that. Quietly. Hockey is, more than anything, a game of cheating without showing it. Otherwise, why would we need referees?"

One can see just how acutely our pitiful genuflecting before the all-powerful video image ignores the essence of the sport. The same thing applies in boxing, where head-butting and elbow shots are illegal, unless it can be done without the referee seeing it. If you think about it, this line of reasoning removes the credibility of video control unless you can add an additional element. Since cheating is a fact of life, on the ground, one can hazard a guess that this process of immediate justice carries within itself the germ of its own transgression. One shivers before the possibilities, not of cheating anymore on the playing field or the court, but of camera fraud. The notion that images might be faked during a supposed live broadcast would require that we film not only the match or the game, but the team that films it in, order to make sure that there was no tampering with the images. And then you also would have to film the guy who films the guy who films the guy who films the guy who films. . .

Which leads us to that remark which is the essence of

amorality, a streetwise bit of wisdom that is less a vow than the basis of any strategy: "In law, it is important to be the first to lie. For nothing is harder for your adversary than to prove that you are lying." Thanks to Mr. C. for this enlightening comment on the subject of jurisprudence. In the morass of rules, the Agité is a cheater. He gets by by ignoring the limits. He crosses the boundaries, into the free zone. And whatever it costs him, that is where he can be free.

Calcutta, India

Dominique Lapierre, the author of *The City of Joy*, is giving a press conference. The local journalists are united, up in arms. They accuse the best-selling writer of having made his fortune on their misery, having damaged the image of Calcutta, of Bengal, of all of India. In the silence that follows these diatribes, Lapierre draws the microphone toward him. With a slow gesture, he draws from his pocket two little bells, the kind that the Calcutta rickshaw drivers sound on the wooden shafts of their carts. It is with this pathetic horn that they try to clear a path through the metal magma of buses and Ambassadors.

"When I walk on Fifth Avenue in New York, on Via Veneto in Rome, the Champs-Élysées in Paris, the Kurfürstendamm in Berlin, in Regent Street in London, everywhere, always, I hold in my hand, at the bottom of my pocket, these bells, which are the heart of Calcutta. And so, with every one of my steps, I hear it beating, beating, beating, the heart, the immense heart of Calcutta." The room is dumbstruck; amazed. And suddenly, it explodes. The irreconcilable enemies of this Westerner are on their feet and applauding, tears in their eyes. Lapierre leans toward me and whispers, "And it goes over even better on the radio."

Close Calls

Seen through the porthole, the view is splendid. In the garnet-red twilight, a cloud of jets passes very close to the fuselage. On the left, on the right, jets emerge, striating the cupola of the sky with the velvety plumes of their twin engines. From our orchestra seats, in "economy" class, we are witnessing (without realizing it) the first steps of the invasion of Kuwait. The Iraqi volley that appears to be escorting us will be blasting bridges and factories. The explosions are lost in the night that is descending upon the Gulf. For the passengers of the planes trapped in the net of Baghdad, months of reclusion will follow. Tourists, businessmen, expats, all of them will be hostages from now on, hostages promoted to the unexpected and unpleasant role of human shield. Our plane took off just in time. We make our way toward India. We barely missed being caught in the scoop.

The journalist and writer Yves Courrière, *Le Figaro*'s special correspondent in Cuba in 1959, says that he had begged his office to grant him an extension. Two or three days extra, because he felt that something was about to happen. In Paris, "the desk" had deduced that this new hire was already trying to take advantage. They held firm, demanded his immediate return. Twenty hours later, in the Paris airport, Yves Courrière, repatriated in spite of himself, learned that Havana was under attack. He too had missed a scoop. He had missed History. If you want to stay close to what's unfolding moment by moment, you have to follow it constantly, and often miss it. The frustration is constant. It prowls. Prescience is a volatile substance, a quick adhesive. When you try to move, it turns out that it has already set. Everything is already over. Much too late.

Some people have a propensity for preceding massive scuffles, riots, the symphony of the riot-guns. I am one of them. It has become a running-gag. When I fly off to any new destination, the watch the newspapers until I get back. The devil as a cyclone, the apocalypse of methane explosions, it's all good for the "front page." After me, the deluge. I barely escaped several major catastrophes, a conflagration in a supermarket, an airplane explosion, earthquake, violent strikes. Splendid disasters. I mention them only because exaltation also comes from this feeling of the close call, when instantaneity takes over. I know what I'm talking about. Barely escaping death stimulates the imagination. No matter what the negatives show, I was in the photograph.

I saw John-Paul I's *Habemus papam*, when he had been pontiff for just a month. I was running, in the very middle of via Conciliazione, amidst a chaos of cornets and joyful cassocks.

The merry clash of the Vatican bells gave a rhythm to the cavalcade. What an exhilarating moment, a legendary event in which the newly elected appeared on the balcony of Saint Peter's Basilica to give his first blessing. I have to admit, it is a holy balcony. We were running, for emotion heaved us like foam on a wave. We were just bubbles. This moment of intense confusion, relayed to the four corners of the universe, and beyond, until the supposed ends of the vault of heaven, it was almost as beautiful as a victory for the Left — with no compromising — a success without the Communist Party. A dream. We ran for this pure act, this act of faith. And we saw everything: cardinals shaking their mitres the way anteaters shake their snouts, a tangle of red velvet on the sacred paving stone, the furious battle that endangered the life of an intrepid newspaper agent. He just had time to hold up his *Osservatore romano* and the sinners attacked him. Dogs on carrion. A very moving spectacle. To save the proletarian's life the Italian police, in all diligence, committed a sacrilegious act and penetrated without a written order, in full uniform, onto Vatican territory. We saw it all, the uniforms trampling on Christian sovereignty but extracting a human being from the rough treatment of the good sisters' shit-kickers. An epic.

We were transported. Blessed by John Paul I, we thought we were invincible. A happy misconception. For the Pope was full of hot air, his staff was nothing but almond paste. And even though we had parked our vehicle in a recess of Trastevere, Romanity was already on the point of penalizing us. The rest is a matter of folklore. Volley and counter volley, a brawl, threats, delinquency, arrest, error, apologies and contrite memories.

We were there. We were no place else. An unexpected departure from Lisbon took us away from the dilapidated Galleria Grandelas. Sad wainscoting in a sad state, empty staircases, tuberculous elevators, yellowing lamps, fires gone out, if I dare say so. We left this universe of memories with a heavy heart. The operetta staircase as well as the ceilings of that store soon were going to disappear under tawdry paintings, smoked mirrors, electronic cameras. Three hours later, while we spun through a furnace of summer toward the desert of Trujillo in Estremadura, the sly dragon of commerce blazed up and released its fumes just like in the pages of Fernando Pessoa.* Its ashes hid the antique district of Chiado under a tide of cinders and for a bit, an attentive soul, coming from the Holy Office and well-versed in the art of the extorting confessions the old fashioned way, would have struck us in the back with this extraordinary fire. Cold sweats in Lusitania.

In other streets, it was Jaipur without a sound. Have you any idea what that means? In this cesspool of a city where phantoms collide, where elephants bang into the mudguards of the starveling pushcart drivers, can you imagine the effect of a crushing silence? A heart attack, murders, passions fanned to a

* A Modernist poet (1888-1935) whose success brought Portuguese literature to the European arena. He wrote his early verse in English.

white heat by Hindus intoxicated with Rama, hapless Moslems disemboweled by the hundreds, marches on the temple of Ayodhya with clubs and spades and daggers and kriss, and the whole thing sanctioned by the army. At the gates of the city, under the pink walls corroded by monsoons and monkeys, the Sikhs in their round turbans, leaning on their "sticks," are holding a conclave in the humidity. In the distance, views of the rosy city. Hawa Mahal deserted. Not a single robber, not even a beggar. But a cow, nonetheless.

Miss the bus, miss everything (or nearly), come to the table but too late. Act reserved, discreet, above all that. Don't allow yourself to be ruffled by dynamite.

The plane from Niamey to Niger and Paris. A hard battle to be treated as VIPs. "Upgrade if avail," the line shone on our ticket stubs. Useless. The crew would hear nothing of it. They were short three seats in first class. We, who had been choking down rotten mutton and struggling with the Jeep for two weeks! We had words. Discourteous exchanges. They won, of course. The next week the flight blew up over the sands of Ténéré. Judge Bruguière is still there, between Tripoli and I don't know where. Everytime I travel, I think about it. Not about the "near miss," but about that flight attendant who would not give in, inflexible, so strict about the rules. A mirage?

New York

Jerry Capeci, four foot ten and wearing a baseball cap, is the only journalist in the world to have a weekly column (in the *Daily News*) on the Mafia. It's called "Gang Land." I ask him whether, hanging out with assassins, he hasn't ended up becoming friends with some of them. He answers, "I don't socialize."

Forgetting

Forgetting. In order to be able to go a little further. To get away from what drags us down. "Existence is a journey in which we have to deal with out baggage," (Emmanuel Levinas.) The coach of sprinter Marie-Jo Pérec explains why for the athlete, it's important not to have a past or a future. Only the present moment must count, entirely crystallized in the will to win. Forget, in order to accelerate. Nietzsche also said it: "One can live with very few memories, but one cannot live without forgetting."

The human limit in racing speed is 300 meters. Beyond that, the body has to break a barrier. As runners approach this wall, they are gradually overcome by panic. Their bodies send danger signals to them: slow down, ease up! They have to be able to block it out entirely, to impose a psychic and muscular deafness. To overcome the fear. When a runner manages to deny his own body's warnings, when he succeeds in breaking this barrier, he feels like he is exploding. Athletes use this expression justly. They pass into another dimension, and this breakthrough, this rebirth, is accompanied for them by the deafening crash of the virtual window that their own body shatters to pieces. The lapse of memory is a detonator, the present is explosive. One can break through to that, one can be reborn through it. That is also the lesson of Agitation, daring to shake the test-tube. Daring to face the sarcastic remarks of the vestals of memory, commemoration and repentance all mixed together. To forget the past it is to be condemned to relive it. Admittedly. But today, that which one forgets, *hic et nunc*, is first and foremost the present. The lesson of the 110-meter hurdle run, flat out, the stress and sweat, the crampons and the cramps, is that stamping out what weighs you down can sometimes allow you to reclaim the present.

Too Lucid

Conversely, too great a clarity can be a problem, too. Overload is always imminent. Wild sudden tsunamis, at any possible moment. A dam that breaks.

There he is, with his hands on Hergé's desk. He is talking, and suddenly, because his voice is putting us to sleep, because the sun that glances off the façades has just slipped onto the carpet, I become aware of everything that surrounds him, of the vertigo and at the same time the smothering sensation generated by the phenomenal accumulation of all the objects in the room. Then the gables of the Hotel de Bruxelles and the gold of the Metropole, through the window, stand out like bright soap bubbles, confounded together with the clouds of powdered sugar puffing up over half-eaten waffles. And the outpouring of this world, because it is so present, becomes unbearable. This extreme perception of totality is overwhelming, overflowing, and there is nothing that can empty it. It is an accumulation, a landslide, the entire universe reduced to a succession of immediacies, time transmuted into a backfire of sparks, the world as a series of lightning bursts, buttressed, thrown in our faces, incandescent slaps, successions of flashes that come so fast they end up losing us. Trapped by having seen too much, destroyed by using the zoom lens so brutally, if pugnaciously.

Another time. Penelope, in a state of hypoglycemia, leaning on Rostand's pedestal in the half-light. At the age of 22 she, and she alone, represents the new wave in French cinema. Fabulous body, heavenly face, and a portfolio with the patina burnished by generations of Sorbonne graduates, dark jacket and slacks, black, grey. The essence of the "intello-morbid" trend. Like the screenwriter Arnaud Desplechin and the writer Jean Rouaud, she has to spend part of her holidays wandering in the chilly cemeteries of the Somme, smitten with an adolescent hardly older than she is. No one has such an inborn talent for choosing her a new black scarf. . . Penelope. No sugar, and no health. She has skipped lunch. She sinks into the dull grumbling of the blood that beats in her temples. She is exhausted but lucid. As though, in the interval that precedes a fainting spell on the terrace, she sensed an urgent need to connect with the world, the urgency of preserving memories of it, to hang onto in case, by chance, she should sink. The clairvoyance of asceticism, the amplitude of the vacuum.

Another time, on the highway between Marseilles and Aix-en-Provence, a Renault, in a Wagnerian flourish, jumps the guardrail and plunges ten feet down into a ditch. Bodies are hauling themselves out of the wreckage. And the driver, struck by a sudden need to dominate, to control whatever is left after his loss of control, is giving orders, legislating, barking. "You, you get over here and you, lie down over there. And you, you take photographs. Help is on the way."

And they all do as they are told, as the astonished rubber-neckers look on; they comply, they lie down. Fabienne, who is still on her feet, walks a few steps and then goes back for her camera to immortalize the entire event. And now the police flood into the disaster scene with a great crash of sliding doors, and while the firemen are dragging out their hoses and training their extinguishers on the smoldering metal carcass, nervous civil servants push back the public and Fabienne, whom they take for a voyeur looking to make trouble for the authorities. In a state of agitation, she shouts for the right to stay with the rest: "But I'm part of the accident! I'm part of the accident!" And all this time, in the mélée and the dust raised by all these soles and souls in turmoil, Guy, lying on the pavement, inert, insensate, almost better than usual, in state of extreme, avid clarity, captures all the words that are being exchanged around him, the crunching gravel, the slamming of the ambulance doors, the stretchers being unfolded; he can't stop thinking about an idiotic sentence that has obsessed him, a sentence he caught one day on some TV program, probably on cable: "When you are dying, you don't feel anything." And that's just it, he doesn't feel bad, he doesn't feel anything and never, oh no, never has he been so lucid in not feeling his body. And that, my God, puts him in a terrible state of anguish!

Taxi drivers spend their time replacing their clutches and the right rear doors, which are slammed all day long, often violently, as if the passenger were seeking vengeance for something. Couldn't they, at least once, switch them with the front right doors or the left-side doors? Have the manufacturers thought about that?

Should I really have noticed that? Why should I worry? Isn't that an inappropriate concern? Isn't that where agitation becomes destructive? Somebody else's toolbox and I am carrying it?

Vertigo, an overdose of observations. A net bloated with jellyfish.

Never Stand Up Straight in an Era That's Bending

Look at things from all sides. Shift around. Agitation must do its part for the Resistance. Distance itself through displacement, by physical travel or word games, by highways or humor.

Stick to the fringes; go off on a tangent. Let the menacing and willful view expand, distorted and contorted, that gives the world back its sense of imagination. We other travelers, scorned by the everyday gurus as transitory comedians already excluded from a planetary matrix, shunted off to a way-station and no longer on the main rails, still savor the poetry of a stop-over. In revolt against the claustrophobia accepted by the majority. No nostalgia for these station-stop cafeterias. No desire to don the tropical helmet, wading boots and mosquito netting (although, as for me. . .), but to seek a correction, within the context of good manners, to all the trembling images that inundate us. Hasn't the slow approach of an elephant become, due to our awareness today of cinematographic technique, a motionless account of how the cameraman was able to make himself invisible, how he managed to disappear? Once you start thinking about the technique, then the line has been crossed. It can be very reassuring, during terribly gory scenes, to say to ourselves, "It's only a movie"; but that also opens up the mind. Understanding how they do it means you also understand what they are doing.

Keep shifting. Pascal Quignard[8] says listening to loud music is a way of recovering the sense of being an animal in a state of alarm, it is putting oneself in the position of being tracked by others, the neighbors whom one may disturb. Be alert. Isn't that also what Gilles Deleuze is saying when he associates culture and coming into contact with other people?

Contact

In his "Alphabet," recorded for distribution after his death, Deleuze took care to differentiate himself from cultivated beings. They, he said, can talk about anything and at any time; not me. He described his method of personal enrichment as "an attitude of being on the lookout." For him, visiting an exhibition, going to a movie or the theater, was to look forward to a meeting somebody. Thinking is, above all, meeting people. Opening shortcuts that, like a cross-tie, keeps the rails balanced. Relationships, connections. How many times I have headed out, armed only with the intuition that, wherever I was going, I would find something, a key. Every time, I set off full of jitters, which grew heavier and heavier, anxious over every penny that my newspaper allowed me for my pursuit. As soon as the plane ticket was in my pocket, the race against the clock began. Then, all the eclecticism of observation was called in as reinforcement. To find something somewhere, anything that could convince my underwriters of my sense of smell. To reassure them. To come through with the goods. Not to return empty-handed.

I find (or better, I encounter) his concept of an investigation, which is a quest more than a conquest, among psychoanalysts in what they describe as "floating listening." It is a state of mystical trance that allows the conscious level of the brain to recognize what usually remains hidden.   It is a quasi-somnambulant state of fuzzy attention, a way of letting resound in oneself something that is born in the remarks of another. A way of collecting in one's mind an explanation that would apply to everything. To some extent, to find something mythical within the lightning flashes.

Listening

In a mimeographed text,[9] Juan David Nasio explains this psychoanalytical listening. He says to allow one's mind to float, to harness itself to whatever the analyst says to him, which will enter into vibration with one of his own hidden thoughts. He bets on the contact, on the current that will awaken in his imagination something that will be able to clarify that of the narrator. In short, he places himself in a position to ensure the transfer, by interposed metaphors, of the myth that we all share.

Sigiria, Sri Lanka

While the temperature rises, we go down. A chaotic, slippery, vertiginous walk on the rock of Sigiria. An old man draped in a kitchen towel slowly climbs toward us. As we meet, he nods his head and, in a voice expressing just a slight, distanced interest, enquires in English, "Satisfied with climbing?"

Calcutta, India

In the strident neon lights of a pistachio-colored dining room, the guests stand up to leave. A very smart Bengali extracts a hand from his *dhoti*, grasps mine and, with heartfelt emotion, lets me know he is "Definitively satisfied."

On Lightning

Then in my turn, I leave it to chance: "Chance, the clothes in which God dresses to present himself to man." Under every latitude, I practice floating listening. In Seattle, day after day I wander about without understanding, along Alaska Way, on the highways that surround Bill Gates' cyberhouse, and on the Microsoft campus; and then it comes, it spouts out, like a bullet, one word extracted, exhumed from the flow of words. "Micro," the word that federates everything, the local microclimate, the micro-weight of Gore-Tex clothing, the microphones of the grunge music scene, the will to preserve a human scale in this exploding city, *"being small, staying small."* . . Micro, micro. . .

And everything is arranged as though it were being seen under a microscope. A gigantic one.

Cochabamba, Bolivia

The old city is separated from the new by a dried up river. Two bridges. On the other side are gaudy restaurants and nightclubs built with cocaine money. In these restaurants where meat is devoured at will, where every diner has ten employees to serve him, where the Mercedes lined up out front are guarded by Chinese men with sunglasses and pistols under their armpits, the families of the *nouveaux riches*, gangsters and traffickers, chow down without a word. Obese women, vulgar men, impudent children itching to be slapped. To get to this neighborhood, just tell a taxi driver: "Barrio narcos." Everyone knows it.

Cochabamba, Bolivia 2

The city is turned to stone. The entire population without exception is nailed down in front of their television sets. The national team of Bolivia is facing the Ecuadorians for the first qualifying round for the "Mundial." A few seconds before the end of the match, as victory finally appears certain, the commentator, who has no voice left, still comes up with the ultimate resource to shout: *"Prepara los petardes!"*[10]

And you have to accept carelessness, too; accept lapses, faux-pas, ink blots. Happy are the dyslexics, heads in the air. Stammering, tongue-twisting, mistaking their wives for hats. Buffoonery. The sleeping bag of ineptitudes. "In the Persia that I had the good fortune to know, the cardinal rule of the caravans. . . was "first step, small step." One only went a *pharsar* (about 4 miles) to give the thoughtless travelers a chance to go back for whatever they might have forgotten."[11] Always leave room for a recovery. A second chance. The dice cup.

In Through the Window

As old militants, natural zapatistas, scout masters and accordion players know, nothing is as good a reinforcement as the conclusion of an alliance. It is worth any argument, any cause, to win the decision. Increasing one's manpower opens every door. It is capital. Growth promotes. It transforms the conspirator into a savior, it catapults him to the role of hero of the day. Who cares if you were vilified, trailed through the mud, called all sorts of names. Where a solitary campaign will denigrate you, a good show with squads of supporters will elevate you, and will launch you to the head of the company. You will be greeted with open arms. You can have the secretariat, the directorship, the central committee.

Even if you have to surrender, always do it in force.

That is a time-honored technique of nepotism. Many political personalities have seen their careers make a spectacular take-off, due to the simple fact that they involved themselves with forces, movements, trends, cliques and clans. They were moved to the first row. Michel Rocard owed his later leadership of the SFIO to his early involvement with the SPF (which brought him into the of the Socialist Party and promoted him through the ranks). The Léo-Lagrange Clubs supported Pierre Maurois, enabling him to impose his powerful stature over the institutions of the same shop. Two examples, two figures who in turn made a Moroccan shine as Prime Minister. Not bad!

That is what is called coming in through the window.

This version of business nomadism contrasts in every way with the more widespread (and thus slower) method of occupying an office. This other approach, more sedentary, the apparatchik's principal technique, consists of first sliding your oxfords under a 100-lb mass of preformed metal. Then, installed in his office like the lightkeeper in his lighthouse, a guy juggles with telephone, keyboard and calculator, day after day. Waiting for time to pass and for his time to come. The person who follow this formula, stuck in front of his in-box, wastes away in the office, and although his room is an individualized universe with a leather desk blotter and a dimmer switch on the halogen lamp, nothing changes; he becomes depressed and spends more time gazing out the window than in dealing with the business at hand. Everything grinds to a standstill. Finally, his "promo" comes. A new office, new lamp, new normality.

The Agité is ill-suited to that approach. He abhors being filed away while he is still alive. For him, "getting in through the window" is an alternative to the façade attack, the direct frontal assault. Cannonballs are more his style, anyway. He gets his strength from being an outsider. To be agitated is, partly, to derive from the outside what will make pressure inside. That requires movement and resourcefulness. To avoid capture, caper and captivate.

Cleary the professional mountaineer (I mean the kind that scales the hierarchies at the risk of a violent fall) has to draw certain obvious conclusions from his attempts at survival in these sniper-infested hills. The forward march is hard. The Agité is at large. He is a conqueror, an invasionary force all unto himself. He waits in ambush, he camps out, he keeps the fires burning. Sometimes the Agité gets burned, himself.

When the harsh winds blow through the treasurers' offices, when the economic indicators start to dip and social programs are being cut back, the ordinary clerk manages to cling to his post while the nomad is out in the first round of cutbacks. That is his lot, the price of his freedom.

Barbarian? For sure. In the fight between the Romanized people and the waves of barbarians, the costume worn by the latter won out over that of the former. The toga, whoever suitable it might be to the Senate and the thermal baths, was replaced by the crude trousers of the rider. Today, some professions retain a sense of pageantry and still assert their homage to the splendors of antiquity: solemn magistrates, lawyers, university professors, popes and multitudes of priests. Jean-Paul Gaultier's tenuous attempts to promote the kilt, viewed as nutty provocations, were actually only a show of allegiance to good Western *ton*. And the *djellaba*, given its similarity to the Roman toga, should give pause to those who are quick to treat those who wear it as savages.

Naples, Italy

Every day, Fabrizio goes to work in the *Questura*, the police prefecture. There he has his little office, his laptop and his telephones. When an attack, a crime or an extortion attempt is announced, he is on the scene as soon as the police are. Describing this very special type of journalist, my comrade photographer F. Zecchin said in his French-Venetian pidgin, "He marches with pistol." In fact, Fabrizio does have a revolver in his belt. Twice, he has tried to use it. The first time, he couldn't get it out of his pants and the second time, he dropped it. He figures he owes his life to these two mishaps.

Dancing

"Nature needs art to extend itself and to keep us from the habit of pure repetition, which is just another form of death. Nature needs to be seen afresh, newly, in the images that we derive from it. It needs to be prolonged, opened out, hatched anew, unceasingly remade and recreated."[12]

Travel, move, jump from one field to another; it's a way of choosing an esthetics of the world. See the quest for innovation as an art form. A creation, a dance (according to Nietzsche, dance was the first art form, a primitive kind of body-writing). Impressions and traces. In this sense, the traveler is a dancer, a practitioner of "density," a dervish, someone who writes the world by traveling it. With the ground as his paper, longitude as his lines, the map of the world as his writing table.

Cunning

To find your way in a foreign city, always trust another foreigner. The Agité on duty helps the Agité passing through, whereas the native is quicker with his mouth than with his mind. *Naturlich!* Any new arrival knows more about a neighbor-hood, a street, a city than the indigenous do. Ask a native for the address of a hotel! What would he know about hotels, he who goes home every night? "The guy on the corner" surveys his territory with his eyes closed. The names of the avenues are less important for him than his memories of certain bars. The émigré house painter from Angola or the Philippines knows his land of adoption like the back of his hand. He has to. And that's the case with all the taxi drivers, Russians one decade, Asians or Africans the next. The fraternity of the lost. Solidarity of the Agités. The birth of art.

Nha Trang, Vietnam

Forty students worried about their next French test have cornered me on the beach. They bombard me with questions from their textbook. "Sir. Do you like to walk along the river on Friday mornings?" Every time, I struggle a little longer. This is idiotic. I can answer anything! I know very well that they don't care about my ideas. What they want is to hear the language of Voltaire! That's all. However, I fence with sincerity. The discussion is awkward. To escape to them, to cut short this test that they are putting me through, I suggest we go have a drink. I motion to a café under the trees, located right at the edge of the beach, less than a hundred yards away. "Not here," answers their ringleader. And why not? "Dear Sir, that is an expensive restaurant." Precisely.

Childhood

In his constantly boiling schizophrenia, the Agité expresses a childhood dream, that of being able to play every side in a game. To be all the characters, to be that willful and lively dandy that Maurice Leblanc, the father of Arsene Lupin, brings to life in his bad novel entitled, with the prescience of Prigogine, *The Fantastic Event*. The hero, although still very young, is showered with rewards. A former athletic champion, he is adored, chased by women and intrigues, rich, spoiled, despoiled and avenged. . . He has seen everything, in twenty-five years. And here he sees, as an eyewitness, the sudden draining of the English Channel. Forget all the nightmares of the Eurotunnel. A ford, a passage pops open between the two nations, sucking up the ferries and steamers as it goes. The power of the serial novel. Reservoir of every possibility.

The biographer Pierre Assouline displays the same characteristic while asserting his friendship with his collaborator Lucien Combelle. Here and there, "I am everywhere." The desire to play all the roles, once again, to be all the characters in the saga. Why should we give up the happiness of pretending? To play is to preserve in oneself the childish part that, in the eyes of others, the vague memory of a poetic union from which we all emerged. To remain a child is, perhaps, to recall in spite of oneself that we were born of the love of others.

Vladimir Jankélévitch: "The true adventurer is always at the beginning." The feeling of never being anywhere but at the start of something, not believing in established positions, secure incomes, authority. Refusing to play the game, when you'd rather laugh at it.

Immaturity, of course; but independence of mind. Rejection of civil imprisonment. Childhood and ants in the pants.

Open the Doors

It'll come as no news to you, if I mention that the universe of the paperback novel is crouching behind every door. In the octopus-like universe of the "glocal" (global + local), there is still a way to get in without following the ironclad law of lobby intercoms. You could ask what buzzer to press, but what good is that? Slipping in behind a pizza delivery man, ducking in as someone else steps out, you have time to glance about and sense the inexhaustible reserve of discoveries, always promised but always put off, and therefore still possible. Every apartment house is a virgin land that remains just that, undeflowered.

"The charm of Proust," writes Roland Barthes in *The Pleasure of the Text*, "is that from one reading to another, you never seem to come across the same passage." The charm of cities. Paragraphs abandoned like forgotten umbrellas. The fascination of doors half-hidden behind partitions, of trap doors hidden under dressers, of cupboards with hidden compartments, secret passages, evanescent corridors, translucent mirrors where the sleepwalker goes through. Everywhere the same infinitude, the same distorted series of events, a paperback novel unfolding at every street corner.

Bikovo, Russia

We're sitting in an airplane with a second-hand propeller, immobilized on the runway here amid the forlorn settlements at the outskirts of Moscow, at an airport that serves "every place that's ugly," according to my interpreter — a big, lugubrious girl who tries to force the door of my hotel room every night. While the cabin is starting to vibrate for a hypothetical takeoff toward Elista, capital of the Autonomous Republic of Kalmykia, a Kalmyk woman is trying to communicate with us in English. She comes up right behind my seat and in a somewhat threatening, accented voice says, "Tovarisch Trétiack. Are you ready?"

"The little soap bubble. . . would not rise, if everything below it were not occupied," (Karl Popper). Behind the apparent vacuum, within the vacuum itself, so much is going on. "It's not that the cord is hanging, it's that the earth is pulling it," wrote Victor Hugo. Same idea, same inversion. Everywhere, behind the light are shadows, and behind the shadows is light. "Shade expresses its hatred of the night and its love of the light," (Nietzsche). The attraction of the funereal, the pugnacity of the interloper. Leonardo da Vinci advised a prolonged study of mold formations, in order to recover the spontaneity of Chinese calligraphy. Mold as the inspiration for freshness. The passion of doors that squeak, of walls that curve, slippery steps. . . cruel architecture, wounded, conscious. Chewed up sidewalks. The sumptuousness of cardboard decorations. The intranquillity of Pessoa, nostalgia for the future, *saudade*. The agitation of the walls, the passion of funeral cities.

"We went down the staircase in an appalling way." How many times have my buddy Pierre Antilogus and I tried to make sense of this sentence by Lovecraft? How do you go down a staircase in an appalling way? On your kidneys, screaming? It must be even worse, for "things that were meant to crawl learned how to walk." Always this *Ausweis* for the House of the Agitated, anteroom or terminus of the popular novel, exoticism of the dark zones. Thugs, assassins, the living dead, weak and noxious creatures, harmful effects of human flesh. Always the cheap novel and its rule of three: any disguised being is unrecognizable; all the principal characters (sworn enemies) are linked, without their knowing it, by blood ties (the assassin is the father of his victim, the monster is the husband of the one he kills, the condemned, the brother of the executioner); finally, and most important, death is never permanent. The dead stay warm and re-appear, bursting with health and a spirit of revenge. This triptych is all it takes for a big trip. The Agité is his own soap opera.

"The Agité of the bottle." Jean-Paul Sartre by Celine. The

supreme compliment. All heavily gilded, carved like the body of a saxophone, a menacing brass horn with a brilliant sound. Under the mustiness, varnish.

Tension

Maurice Leblanc, again. I am sure that he, who ended his life in his manor at Étretat, duly protected from the possible escapades of his hero by a zealous police force, never envisaged the success of the title of his novel *813*. Fans of crime novels made a cult around it and the number keeps cropping up, fantastically, phantasmagorically. What's the big deal? The female effect of the bodies of the figures 3 and 8 frame the entirely masculine 1; and there is an additional, subtler, and frankly medical quality. 813 is, literally, the ideal tension ratio. A patient with a blood pressure reading of 13/8 is in perfect physical condition. Reversed, this 13/8 becomes, to some extent, a sign of suppressed health, a restrained effect, a dis-tension. A retention. 8/13. Not exactly hypotension but a kind of ill in-tension.

Worse. A blood pressure reading that doesn't end, or doesn't really start: an 8 without the 13. An assumption of low blood pressure that nothing can raise. Waiting, while the blood slips into the veins and drains out, permanently; waiting in the hope of hearing a second "beep!" that is deferred forever. Now, that is attention. In short, agitation in concentration. A great art.

Exile Yourself

If the door doesn't open, slap the map. Leave.

A gloomy wait in Falls Road, Belfast. The day before, the bullet of the return whistled past our ears. The retreat toward Paris was heralded loud and clear. Six hours of interviews at the Sinn Féin headquarters, sitting between a couple of toughs with faces like pirates, had left me without a trace; neither notes nor a hint of an idea. Not a single line. I had nodded my head, acquiescing to the volcanic outpouring of words, accounts of rapes in the cell, ambushes at the factory exit, unemployment transmitted from generation to generation. I had not stopped them on any point.

That evening, huddled in the car under the usual fine rain, we stopped to ask directions of the only guy in the area — a tall guy in cigarette pants, he appeared on the moor, propelled by his fluorescent green socks. A deathblow. Like a rubber bullet, his "Yojosstönnereèèèktyokeütmêêsset!"[13] struck us dumb, and the moment of shocked silence that followed earned us the ritual question: "Yo dan't speekkk aaanglish?" Since this was now quite difficult for us to answer credibly, we felt our morale and our legs go limp. We suddenly felt cramped inside our metallic shell.

Fortunately, there were pints of beer to help us get back in the saddle and to muffle the uproar of our ulcers. In Northern Ireland (and no doubt throughout all of Ireland) the food is so poor that one has to be desperate to tolerate it. Franco Z, our Venetian nomad, has his own way of dealing with it. He brings his own seasoning. Anywhere in the world, from bar to brasserie, at mealtime he pulls out of the "film" pocket of his photographer's jacket an empty plastic Kodachrome 64 film container. That's where he keeps his powder, crushed hot red pepper flakes, and he sprinkles all his food with it, every meal that is undefinable and always suspect. This red napalm obliterates bacteria, overrides disgusting aromas, neutralizes all other flavors. It is the powder in the powder kegs. It's an excellent idea, except for those who wear contacts — for once it gets under your nails, this pepper that is supposed to exalt the dullest shoe leather smothered in gluey sauce gets into your eyeballs and drives them crazy. It is an exotic form of myxomatosis.

Spices

The spices always have to be hotter and hotter, and travelers can get burned using this tactic. After a few years, the mustard method doesn't work anymore. I could feel that my palate was tanned like leather, hardened, armored. In fact, my teeth were no longer accompanied by agitated tastebuds but by steel-reinforced concrete, which was rusting. As the callus transforms the plantar area of the foot into a hardened rubber sole, the peppers, *harissa*, curry and other blends of Malaysian spice line the oral orifice and its dependences. It is fire in the mouth. I know some who have paid dearly. Personally, it was a "deviled chicken" consumed at the Beach Paradise in Mirissa, Sri Lanka, that did me in. It came back, fiber for fiber, throughout the entire course of an apocalyptic intestinal transit. At every point of passage, the bolus announced its contents and asserted itself. From tongue to esophagus, stomach, intestine, and further, if you'll follow me to the epicenter, the pain carved a deeper trench.

Rare is the traveler who can still savor the ectoplasmic charms of a gooey chop suey, of a turnip in juice, of a broad bean in *court bouillon*. Ingesting the scrapings of tropical subsoil is more like sucking venom from a wound than sucking candy! How, then, can we blame our larynxes when they revolt? Sometimes, too much is too much. The body rebels. Fever and vomiting are nothing compared to this spectacle, mere spring showers compared to this tornado! No, the real convulsion that explodes, fills the room and empties the cupboards, that is something else altogether. One afternoon in Delhi, while waiting for a flight to Kathmandu (another obligatory goal for any serious Agité), I felt that the accumulation of *chapati* with onions, the *vindaloo* and other *tikkas* glowing with paprika, the curries wadded together into Everest mounds of explosive, suddenly joined forces and rose up against their host. It was my head that caught fire first. For a few hundred yards, wandering around in the vicinity of the tomb of Humayun Sikandar Lodi, I staggered from fountain to faucet, not to drink the brackish and miasmic water but to rain it upon my cranium and the nape of my neck.

The temperature kept changing, ebbing one moment and surging again a few steps further down the trail. By evening, matters had only gotten worse. Far worse! Sweats, the shakes, everything was poured out into the alchemy of confused vocabulary, where "chilly" was swapped with "chili" and vice versa, in a hash of aromatics.[14] I had long since laid down, waiting for all this to pass; but was "it"? Around ten o'clock that evening, the odor woke me up. On first glance my bed seemed to have become a wading pool, overhung by a cloud smelling of greasy sweat and saffron. I had the dreadful conviction that barefooted servants, some kind of evil-doers, had deliberately brought my bed into the kitchen. It was as if the hotel was frying, roasting, baking, breading and battering truckloads of chicken and pork in my cramped little bedroom. The emanations of curry prowled alongside the bed, clambered up the curtains. And all that was exhaled from my spongiform body. All the curry that had accumulated for three weeks was trying to escape through my pores, my body that had gone from serving as an envelope to resembling more a shroud; or, more precisely, my cells in a desperate maneuver had finally banded together to expel this foreign agent that was threatening to break apart the entire edifice. I was corroding, and my body, in a heroic act of resistance, came to the rescue of the mind that had put it in danger. I cried tears of tamari, pools of basmati rice, lakes of chicken muglai, oceans of masala. For the next six months, the mere sight of a crystallized lemon or a banana chutney, if it bore the trademark of a supplier of the Raj, would give me contractions of the bowels. And what do you think I did? Like an addict, I went back. I wandered back to neighborhood of the spice shops on a beautiful day, I found my way through the bazaars, to taste, at the end of a fork, the carbonized end of a bamboo skewer and, from admission to confession, I ended up inserting (without the least remorse) myriads of halberds into my stomach, while waiting for my immune defenses to reboot, or begin their final breakdown. Pepper always wins out over the globe-trotter. A sign of the times

Coffee

It was Ali Ben Oman Al-Shadil, a Sufi Yemeni, who propagated the use of coffee throughout Happy Araby. Since then, we know that there are some grinds that are more grinding than others, that buck and kick. All the same, while it is reasonable to disdain a Dutch *Lavasse*, perfectly acceptable to complain about American coffee even though it is so heavily promoted these days, there is one mishap that any Agité inevitably will face sooner or later. At coffee time, when he should call out, "Turkish coffee!," suddenly he hesitates. Isn't it, rather, Greek coffee? And isn't the lackey springing toward your table between two walls of *kadaïfs* going to take it badly if, by chance, you commit an unpardonable error? In the Moskva Hotel in Belgrade, at the height of the "Studenski protests" in the winter of 1997, I had the misfortune of being reprimanded by a waiter, delicately expansionist, who curtly interrupted me when I ordered a "*double turkish coffee*," in strict accordance with the menu itself, where it was inscribed, black on white: *Turkawa Kaffa.* "*Yes, sir. But it is not Turkish coffee. It is Serbian coffee.*" I have also heard that a Muslim in Sarajevo, a great manipulator of arabica, uses the surrealist name of "*Bosnian coffee.*" In the same vein, when I mention this incident to coffee-grind specialists who wear a tarboosh, a chechia or a fez, I have been advised that in Syria it is better to banish any "Turkish" at all from one's vocabulary. It seems that, in the outskirts of Damascus, as well as in the Lebanese plain of Bekaa, it goes over very well indeed if you order, authoritatively, an "*oriental coffee.*" Of course, we could all just switch to tea to ensure harmony.

How exciting it is to visit the battery chargers: London, New York, the Cape, Shanghai, Mumbai, Austin, Rotterdam. . . everywhere that people walk at a run, where the body inflates and hums like a power station. To extract oneself from the inert matrix where nothing new is said or done. To breathe in all kinds of deviant speech, originality and surprise, to risk short-circuiting, to stay in the race, feet on the pavement, fundamentally tuned in.

An irrepressible attraction for the hells on earth. Rows of miners' cottages, polluted zones, massacres, Silesia, the Aral Sea, New Delhi, Dacca; collective suicide, blue clouds of gasoline, handkerchiefs blackened with sooty compounds, emanations of sulphur, rotten eggs, petrochemicals infiltrating the very corridors of the hotel, penetrating the restaurants, creeping under the mats, oozing into the operating room. Industrial miasmas. Dante on the horizon, every morning, every minute. At every step. The uncontrollable exaltation of the dive into dullness and ugliness. Belgrade, Sofia, in dirty snow, hunching low over the icy crust.

Later, as the plane flies over the outskirts of Frankfurt, the absurd feeling that someone should use a vacuum cleaner on the autobahn.

With Pavel Lunghin, filming *Luna Park*. In Moscow's biggest working foundry. A pile of ruins, smashed iron and steel castings. Metal heaps, dangerous, sharp, threatening, in equilibrium, like carcasses of steam locomotives ramming each other. Ramming at full speed. "You would think the factory was bombed yesterday." "You imbecile!" Pavel shouts to me above the racket. "You don't understand anything! This factory is bombed every day!"

Bangkok

Every real traveler sooner or later deposits his bag at the edge of the blacktop at the airport in Bangkok. An obligatory port of call in Asia, crossroads of the sub-continent, Bangkok presents itself above all as a straight line forcefully slammed on top of a revolting disorder. Even though the traffic may be a little less congested than before, if you floor your Subaru you can still cut in two one of those yellow dogs nosing around in an insane appreciation of mechanics. When it goes "crack" under the wheels, the driver, vaguely annoyed, casts a glance in the rearview mirror, catches the eye of the European who is distressed by such a non-event, shrugs a shoulder and says, *"What can I do? Nothing!"* Indeed, in this iron lung of a city compressed from the interior, you can't, strictly speaking, do anything. A Scots photographer who oxidized the cells of his respiratory system by spending a few weeks in the pandemonium of the Thai capital lets lose a tirade that closes the subject. "Bangkok: the only city which I have physically felt growing, all around me." Just so. As another photographer complained, while venting (or was it the other way around?) *"We used to have spring and summer. Now we only have HOT."* Meanwhile, they have filled in the *klongs* (stagnating canals), cut down the trees, re-tooled tri-cars into dump trucks, and poured tons and tons of concrete to erect buildings that absorb the heat through their foundations and spit it out from all their balconies, verandas, ventilation shafts, elevators, air-conditioners and stairwells. Bangkok!

The first night you're there, like everyone else, you go to Pat Pong. "You have to see everything, so you can say you did." A good excuse. For six dollars at the door, you can get a face full of the contortions of a girl who threads bananas into her vagina in order to expel them, with a squeeze of the kidneys, onto the hapless tourists positioned in the first row by tour leaders on commission. The unfortunate soul who shows up wearing a tie can be sure he'll see it disappear, right up to the allegorical knot, in the geisha muck of the one whose two thighs have caressed his moustache. In short, between two rows of razor blades you-know-where and a beer guzzled at the counter, hair frizzing in the heat under the gluteus halo of Go-Go girls, one has his dose of Bangkok nightlife.

And then, there is the daytime. And it is worse. The sex has nothing to do with the general sense of catastrophe, it's just the caboose. A monumental diarrhea of metal and rubble. In a few years' time, the entire city has taken on the aspect of a con-glomeration of construction sites. It is almost as though they were constantly trying to stick to the back of a truck overloaded with sacks of cement, some of which gradually release clouds of their contents onto the cars that follow them. Heat and dust. It is so ugly that it starts to grow on you. We've all heard about the vehicles transformed into offices with all the comfort of modern hygiene, all heard about the traffic jams where you are trapped in your steel coffin. We've heard all that. And yet, it's not really like that. It's always worse.

Spark-Plug Engines

It is true that Bangkok is a toy chest. PIA, Biman, Burma Airways, Cathay Pacific, tight rows of counters spit out their plane tickets. This is where I broke my own record. Nine means of transportation in the course of a day and three border crossings. Departure at dawn from Vientiane, to Laos, in an internal combustion tripod *tuk-tuk*. Two miles, and we have combustion, indeed! A breakdown on the shoulder. *Baksheesh*, mighty efforts, pushing, set out again humming, and the river edge is in sight. A boat of reinforced wicker. High emotions, between gangs of kids and piles of bundles. Attack by Thai custom officials. Waltz of the rubber stamps, and re-*tuk-tuk* (this time, in the high-wheeled kind), transmission crackling, hopping on six terminals. A stop at the snack stand, get a ticket, the oars are raised, wooden benches, window on the flags waving, wind in the sails, collapse, heat. A whistle, and the ticket terminal. Bangkok. Scuffle on the quay, re-re-*tuk-tuk* taking the Sukhumvit Road option and its metallic nightmare. An automobile showroom every three hundred yards. Now we come to Air-Vietnam. Offices upstairs, every modern inconvenience. Carnivorous smiles, real socialism, dollars accepted here. Banknotes in Bangkok, inclination as a way of expressing disinclination, and fork over something extra. 600 bucks! A fortune. At least, and at last, after about a dozen phone calls upstairs, with stomach churning and cigarettes burning. At any rate, two new visas burning bright as coal on our passports and re-re-re-*tuk-tuk* to a taxi, to the airport, to Singapore via Biman (the Bangladeshi airline, for anyone who doesn't know — lucky devil) and there (Holy Father, Vishnu of the islands, Ali Pasha pray for us) a stop in a health resort, Singapore, the Switzerland of the tropics, all nickel and odeon, trees all freshly vacuum-cleaned, very beautiful, spick and span, cops everywhere. Taxis with roof lights to keep them from speeding. Stop at Raffles, the legendary hotel and our reward. Hit the stopwatch: nine conveyances to make it to an air-conditioned room. Can you beat that, big traveler?

A final echo. Everything is agitated, the whole planet is rustling. The world buzz.

Havana, Cuba

To torment Leonardo, our guide, we keep asking him the same question. "Octavio, what were you doing while the *Barbudos* were fighting in the Sierra?" Then Leonardo fidgets in his seat, twists his hands, adopts a casual air and says, "Oh, me, I wasn't really conscious ("*conciencia*") at the time." We like this story of "*conciencia*" a lot; it sounded so funny in this ruined country. Fifteen years later, we don't like it any more. It even seems rather sordid, our good little joke. We are having a belated pang of *conciencia*.

Always take notes, mark up the reference book, asterisks, brackets, notes and erasures. General penetration, gangrene, subversion. Vertigo, when the context exceeds the text.

"Always write the foreword of the book, after the book. . . in order to be able to disavow the book" (Levinas). Never rest.

Finally, to conclude, to put an end to this agitation. To

bring to a close this endless rampage that, like a wave, sweeps up everything in its path. Everything that happens is grasped, spat out, marked. I would like to exhaust the subject, but it is the subject that is likely to exhaust us. So then, better to shake well before using. Done.

And now, we are ready to use it. Like carpet cleaner. Idiotic and uninhibited supercharger.

Dervishes, Agités, antizappers and irreproachable. Have I convinced you of the beauty of always going full tilt? Doubt overwhelms me, knocks at my heart. A new agitation, the agitation of doubt.

Continuity and discontinuity. QED.

A motto that will never lead you astray: shoot your quarry before you finish pissing.

Footnotes

1. "Our vitality fluctuates so much between mystical trance and complete depression because of a fundamental error that we make about the nature of our consciousness. We think that it is a reflex, like breathing. That is wrong; it involves an effort like swimming. If we stop making that effort, we sink." (Colin Wilson, cited by M. G. Dantec in *tLes Racines du mal*, Serie noire, Gallimard, p. 391.)

2. "Children use their mouths to mimic the sounds that adults produce, and from this ludic imitation is born actual human language. Admittedly, they also make cries of alarm. The ludic use of cries of alarm leads to the first lie. And thus the problem of truth appears. And with the problem of truth, also the problem of representation. . . Language arises because one cries "Wolf!," in jest, and in so doing, one lies. That is the moment when the problem of truth is born, and with it, the problem of representation. The problem of truth exists only in connection with representation. For honeybees, there is no problem of truth. . . they are not able to lie." (Karl Popper, *L'Avenir est ouvert*, Flammarion, p. 45.) Nothing is more false than sworn oaths.

3. "Dissymmetry," in R. Caillois, *Coherences aventureuses*, Idées/Gallimard, p. 193.

4. Jean-Luc Godard, interview with Jean Hatzfeld in *Liberation* (1996).

5. Nicolas Bouvier, *L'Echappee belle*, op. cit., p. 18.

6. "I stammer. All my words are worn down; you would think that I place them at random." (Dostoyevsky, *The Brothers Karamazov*, Livre de poche, p. 149.)

7. Michel Pastoureau, *L'Etoffe du diable. Une histoire des rayures et des tissus rayes*, Le Seuil.

8. Pascal Quignard, *Hatred of the music*, Calmann-Lévy, p. 21.

9. Juan David Nasio, "How a psychoanalyst works."

10. "Get those firecrackers ready!" (And/or "farts," coincidentally.)

11. Nicolas Bouvier, *L'Echappee belle, op. cit.*, p. 85.

12. Charles-Ferdinand Ramuz, *Remarques*, L'Age de l'Homme, p. 31.

13. "You just turn right you can't miss it." . . . with an accent.

14. Octavio Paz, who was Mexican Ambassador to India, noted that the two nations shared the same eccentric enthusiasm for pepper. "The Spanish word *chile* comes from *nahua*, the Aztec language. The plant originated in America." In the same vein, Octavio Paz remarked that

Indians and Mexicans also shared a love of thin, wafer-like breads (*chapati* and *tortilla*), of white tunics (the *china problana* and the *dhoti*), and of pyramidal religious architecture. (Octavio Paz, *Lueurs de l'Inde*, Gallimard Arcades, p. 91 sq.)

Also from Algora Publishing:

CLAUDIU A. SECARA
THE NEW COMMONWEALTH
From Bureaucratic Corporatism to Socialist Capitalism

The notion of an elite-driven worldwide perestroika has gained some credibility lately. The book examines in a historical perspective the most intriguing dialectic in the Soviet Union's "collapse" — from socialism to capitalism and back to socialist capitalism — and speculates on the global implications.

IGNACIO RAMONET
THE GEOPOLITICS OF CHAOS

The author, Director of *Le Monde Diplomatique*, presents an original, discriminating and lucid political matrix for understanding what he calls the "current disorder of the world" in terms of Internationalization, Cyberculture and Political Chaos.

TZVETAN TODOROV
A PASSION FOR DEMOCRACY –
Benjamin Constant

The French Revolution rang the death knell not only for a form of society, but also for a way of feeling and of living; and it is still not clear as yet what did we gain from the changes.

MICHEL PINÇON & MONIQUE PINÇON-CHARLOT
GRAND FORTUNES –
Dynasties of Wealth in France

Going back for generations, the fortunes of great families consist of far more than money—they are also symbols of culture and social interaction. In a nation known for democracy and meritocracy, piercing the secrets of the grand fortunes verges on a crime of lèse-majesté . . . *Grand Fortunes* succeeds at that.

CLAUDIU A. SECARA
TIME & EGO –
Judeo-Christian Egotheism and the Anglo-Saxon Industrial Revolution

The first question of abstract reflection that arouses controversy is the problem of Becoming. Being persists, beings constantly change; they are born and they pass away. How can Being change and yet be eternal? The quest for the logical and experimental answer has just taken off.

JEAN-MARIE ABGRALL
SOUL SNATCHERS: THE MECHANICS OF CULTS

Jean-Marie Abgrall, psychiatrist, criminologist, expert witness to the French Court of Appeals, and member of the Inter-Ministry Committee on Cults, is one of the experts most frequently consulted by the European judicial and legislative processes. The fruit of fifteen years of research, his book delivers the first methodical analysis of the sectarian phenomenon, decoding the mental manipulation on behalf of mystified observers as well as victims.

JEAN-CLAUDE GUILLEBAUD
THE TYRANNY OF PLEASURE

The ambition of the book is to pose clearly and without subterfuge the question of sexual morals -- that is, the place of the forbidden -- in a modern society. For almost a whole generation, we have lived in the illusion that this question had ceased to exist. Today the illusion is faded, but a strange and tumultuous distress replaces it. No longer knowing very clearly where we stand, our societies painfully seek answers between unacceptable alternatives: bold-faced permissiveness or nostalgic moralism.

SOPHIE COIGNARD AND MARIE-THÉRÈSE GUICHARD
FRENCH CONNECTIONS –
The Secret History of Networks of Influence

They were born in the same region, went to the same schools, fought the same fights and made the same mistakes in youth. They share the same morals, the same fantasies of success and the same taste for money. They act behind the scenes to help each other, boosting careers, monopolizing business and information, making money, conspiring and, why not, becoming Presidents!

VLADIMIR PLOUGIN
RUSSIAN INTELLIGENCE SERVICES. VOL. I. EARLY YEARS

This collection contains the latest works by historians, investigating the most mysterious episodes from Russia's past. All essays are based on thorough studies of preserved documents. The book discusses the establishment of secret services in Kievan Rus, and describes heroes and systems of intelligence and counterintelligence in the 16th-17th centuries. Semen Maltsev, a diplomat of Ivan the Terrible's times is presented as well as the much publicised story of the abduction of "Princess Tarakanova".

JEAN-JACQUES ROSA
EURO ERROR

The European Superstate makes Jean-Jacques Rosa mad, for two reasons. First, actions taken to relieve unemployment have created inflation, but have not reduced unemployment. His second argument is even more intriguing: the 21st century will see the fragmentation of the U. S., not the unification of Europe.

DOMINIQUE FERNANDEZ
ROMANIAN RHAPSODY

"Romania doesn't get very good press." And so, renowned French travel writer Dominique Fernandez heads out to form his own images.

ANDRÉ GAURON
EUROPEAN MISUNDERSTANDING

Few of the books decrying the European Monetary Union raise the level of the discussion to a higher plane. European Misunderstanding is one of these. Gauron gets it right, observing that the real problem facing Europe is its political future, not its economic future.

EDITOR: BERNARD-HENRI LÉVY
WHAT GOOD ARE INTELLECTUALS?
44 Writers Share Their Thoughts

Interviews with Nadine Gordimer, Ivan Klima, Arthur Miller, Czeslaw Milosz, Joyce Carol Oates, Cynthia Ozick, Octavio Paz, Salman Rushdie, Susan Sontag, William Styron, Mario Vargas Llosa and others.

PAUL LOMBARD
VICE & VIRTUE
Men of History, Great Crooks for the Greater Good

Paul Lombard unearths the secrets of the corridors of power. He reveals the vanity and the corruption, but also the grandeur and panache that characterize the great. This cavalcade over many centuries can be read as a subversive tract on how to lead.

RICHARD LABÉVIÈRE
DOLLARS FOR TERROR
The U.S. and Islam

"In Labévière's riveting, often shocking analysis, the U.S. is an accessory in the rise of Islam, because it manipulates and aids radical Moslem groups in its short-sighted pursuit of its economic interests, especially the energy resources of the Middle East and the oil- and mineral-rich former Soviet republics of Central Asia. — This important book sounds a wake-up call to U.S. policy-makers."

—*Publishers Weekly*

JEANNINE VERDÈS-LEROUX
DECONSTRUCTING PIERRE BOURDIEU
Against Sociological Terrorism From the Left

Sociologist Pierre Bourdieu went from widely criticized to widely acclaimed, without adjusting his hastily constructed theories. Turning the guns of critical analysis on his own critics, he was happier jousting in the ring of (often quite un-democratic) political debate than reflecting and expanding upon his own propositions.

HENRI TROYAT
TERRIBLE TZARINAS

Who should succeed Peter the Great? Upon the death of this visionary and despotic reformer, the great families plotted to come up with a successor who would surpass everyone else — or at least, offend none. But there were only women — Catherine I, Anna Ivanovna, Anna Leopoldovna, Elizabeth I. These autocrats imposed their violent and dissolute natures upon the empire, along with their loves, their feuds, their cruelties.

JEAN-MARIE ABGRALL
HEALERS OR STEALERS
Medical Charlatans

Fear of illness and death: are these the only reasons why people trust their fates to the wizards of the pseudo-revolutionary and the practitioners of pseudo-magic? check their powers of judgment at the door. Jean-Marie Abgrall is Europe's foremost expert on cults and forensic medicine.